Customer Experience without Borders
A Practical Guide to Social Media in Financial Services

By Christophe Langlois

First published 2011 by Searching Finance Ltd, 8 Whitehall Road, London W7 2JE, UK

ISBN: 978-1-907720-15-4

Typeset by: Deirdré Gyenes

Customer Experience without Borders
A Practical Guide to Social Media in Financial Services

By Christophe Langlois

About Christophe Langlois

Christophe is an advisor, blogger, speaker, event organizer and business networker. He spent most of his career in banking and financial services covering the EMEA region.

Over the last four years, Christophe established himself as one of the most trusted advisors to the financial services industry on the topics of social media, voice of the customer, and advocacy. He is passionate about people and focused on finding ways by which a traditionnal and serious industry can better engage with its market, its employees and its clients on digital channels such as online and mobile.

Christophe is an experienced presenter, thought leader, and advocate for social media and customer experience in financial services, and he is a regularly requested chairperson and speaker at conferences.

Since 2007, Christophe has contributed to over 50 events in 12 countries.

Before working at Lloyds TSB, one of the major banks in the UK, as Head of Online Sales then Senior Innovation Manager, Christophe worked in international business development, in both telecommunications and banking. In these roles he helped drive significant new business in both the payments straight through processing, and anti-money laundering space.

About Visible Banking

In 2007 Christophe founded Visible-Banking.com, which quickly became the leading independent blog 100% focused on social media in banking, financial services and insurance.

At Visible Banking we help financial institutions all over the world to better understand and leverage social media in a strategic yet pragmatic way. We focus on all the areas of financial services applied to B2C, B2B and B2B2C environments.

We deliver the following services:

- **Learning & Benchmarking:** we design and deliver bespoke internal seminars, coaching or training sessions as well as external events. As of April 2011, we successfully delivered 5 workshops in London, Paris, Madrid and Singapore. We provide our clients with regular industry updates, benchmarks and reports.
- **Consulting:** we conduct social media audits with pragmatic recommendations, we help our clients design their social media strategy and take their existing initiatives to the next level. We coach community managers and enable them to design easily actionable content strategies. Know Your Followers/Fans-KYF strategy: we help our clients better understand and fully leverage their communities on services like twitter or facebook.
- **Connecting:** we facilitate introductions (business development) and conversations between financial institutions and the most innovative startups and companies in social media, engagement banking, the voice of the customer and online finance.

The Visible Banking Team now tracks over 2,400 initiatives from financial institutions in 70+ countries on Twitter, Facebook, YouTube and blogs (April 2011). We constantly use our unique data to provide the most insightful recommendations to our clients.

We invite you to join the conversation on:

- The Visible Banking blog (http://Visible-Banking.com)
- The Visible Banking Facebook page (http://Facebook.com/VisibleBanking)
- The Visible Banking Twitter account (http://Twitter.com/Visible_Banking)

A Customer Experience Without Borders
An occasional series of books, checklists, reports, and white-papers exploring the developing role of social media in global financial services.

Title 1: A Practical Guide to Social Media in Financial Services

Title 2: I am thinking about putting together some books on Facebook and Twitter, do you think this is a good idea?

Please feel free to send me any comments or ideas to christophe.langlois@visible-banking.com.

About Searching Finance
Searching Finance Ltd is a dynamic new voice in knowledge provision for the financial services and related professional sectors. Our mission is to provide expert, highly relevant and actionable information and analysis, written by professionals, for professionals. For more information, please visit www.searchingfinance.com

Contents

Chapter 2 Leadership, senior executives and social media... **39**

Chapter 7 Turning your clients into loyal brand ambassadors: voice of the customer and transparency

Customer Experience without Borders

xiv

Customer Experience without Borders

Acknowledgements

I'd like to dedicate this book to my parents, Gérard and Nelly Langlois, and my fiancée, Katie Tobin, for their unconditional support and love.

Without their help and their understanding, I wouldn't have been in a position to invest so much time and energy on Visible-Banking.com, and spend nights and weekends sharing my passion for social media and engagement banking with my peers.

And now, after four years of regular blogging and 50-something public speaking engagements all over the world, comes this book.

Introduction

I am a big believer in transparency in business and have no time for smoke and mirrors – what's the point?

Therefore I think that it is only right that I declare that this book that you hold in your hand, or read on your Kindle, or view as a pdf on some other device, is an excellent collection of best practices, actionable insights and pragmatic recommendations.

But customer expectations and behaviours are changing every day. Social media is a live and learn approach, so it is fundamental your organisation start building its presence, engaging with your customers, and leveraging this book asap. Be prepared to make mistakes and more importantly, be prepared to learn from your mistakes. I'm confident this book will help you save time and maximize the success of your social media initiatives from the very first try.

The ROI of social media: your business will still exist in five years

As someone who is fascinated by social media and has tracked it closely for several years now, across some 70 different countries, I know that there are new initiatives launched daily, new usage patterns, new apps, new everything emerging all the time. At the moment, for example, there are lots of rumours about social media companies and payments. I am also aware that there are initiatives losing momentum and stopping all the time; today's big launch isn't always in operation in a year's time. What seems innovative today won't be in six months … so I realise that in the time between the completion of my writing, and the book ending up in your hand, things will have changed.

Social media is exciting and ever developing. As political upheaval occurred in North Africa and the Middle East and we witnessed the horror of the Japanese earthquake, new and innovative uses of social media have emerged. Perhaps I will document these in my next book …

It is becoming ever more critical for any financial institution to ensure employees learn how to connect with customers with the right tone of voice. You must increase your capacity as an organization to adapt to growing customer expectations and prepare for the next generation of communication channels. Get ready for the world after Facebook or Twitter.

Social media is all about people, not technology. Internally, it is very much a matter of change management. Are banks and insurance firms ready to be more transparent, let their employees express themselves publicly, give a voice to their customers, come what may?

The enduring value of books

Even more importantly, social media is a spirit and an approach. It is an experience, not just a set of tools or sites to visit or content to download. How does one capture this intangible spirit? Collaborating, sharing, experiencing, engaging. Part of me is doubtful that these qualities can be described fully in a traditional medium such as a book. So why do I bother? And what is "my call to action"? (Do you like this expression? I hope so, as you will be hearing it a lot!) Well, I am in fact a great fan of the printed word and I think that books still have much value.

Books are a wonderful way for curators to aggregate all the most relevant and valuable content about a topic in one single place. If it seems that it is less fashionable these days to spend a significant amount of time in one writers' company, I think we lose something (for one thing our attention span) if our whole time is spent just clicking from one thing, to the next. Understanding social media is as much about appreciating nuance as it is about anything else, and this is best built slowly.

The relationship between my blog and my book

In this book, the first in the series, I offer the chance to stand back and reflect on the material that I have assembled (perhaps with your help if you are one of the visitors to my site) from my blogging, my seminars, and what I have observed in the social media world over the past five years.

Let me be very clear about this: my book does not simply collect and reproduce my blog entries in date or theme order – what would be the use of that?

You can go and refer to them as they are, yes?

Rather I have attempted to distil the principles from what I have researched and observed (although as I have already said social media is constantly in flux). I think enough has now happened in the industry to write a manual of best practice.

In writing this, I have found myself referring back to material and observations from a few years ago, as well as my more recent work. Although technology dates, the underlying principles of what makes for a successful community don't.

How best to capture the spirit of social media?

But one thing I am uneasy about is that, like any book, this is essentially one person's account, whereas the beauty of social media is that it creates the means for continuous dialogue, debate and interaction. The variety of media involved (audio, visual and touch) allows for ever richer experiences that can stimulate the senses and create real engagement.

In my seminars I am always looking to create energy and bounce, and I have tried to bring this approach to my book. How?

Well, I am constantly asking questions throughout the text, to which I hope you will take time to respond (to me or to yourself). If you have this book in electronic format you can click to my site at any point and post your thoughts or view some of the original source material.

I have also tried to write in a way that is punchy and incisive and recognises that you are probably a very busy person.

As much as possible I have broken up the text with bullets and used a colloquial style. I am very grateful for your views on whether this style works or not, and if I should use it in the other projects in this series? Feedback please! I am not one to hold back when I think others can improve, so be harsh, but be truthful. I look forward to hearing from you!

So what is in this book?

It is:

- ◆ a best practice guide;
- ◆ a start-up guide;
- ◆ a wake-up call to those who have tried their best to imagine that social media never happened, or is only relevant to other people;
- ◆ a guide to recruiting and working with (and not against) your social media team;
- ◆ a guide to the commonly made mistakes (and how to avoid them);
- ◆ a guide to some of the more challenging questions you need to be asking to a social media software vendor (trust me, you can have fun with this);
- ◆ a guide to those aspects of social media whose importance is typically underestimated;

- a dictionary of key terms and concepts (some of them my own);
- a guide to judging and assessing your social media operation;
- a breakdown of best practice by banking market and segment;
- perhaps the most comprehensive financial social media case book ever assembled;
- a proof of the business case and return on investment (ROI) from social media (lend a copy to your Chief Financial Officer);
- a guide to managing talent, improving worker relations, breaking silos and achieving a ROI;
- an opportunity to learn the lessons and assess the contribution of those who didn't execute their initiatives properly (I make these comments with absolutely no desire to cause ill feeling, and I hope that it will be seen as so); but I do feel that these examples often present the best learning points.
- the history of an emerging (although some might describe it as an established) form of communication and a tribute to the individuals and companies that pioneered and innovated in social media (amid the scepticism);
- and, of course, a forecast of where the industry might go next.

Above all, the one theme that I hope emerges, from every sentence of the book, is how to create an ever greater customer experience.

Each chapter of the book has been designed to be read as a standalone, although naturally I hope you will read the whole thing!

Once again I must be transparent...there is a very simple shortcut through the book, and it involves understanding one word – reward. Ok perhaps I'm exaggerating, two words, reward and engage. If you truly understand what these words mean and how to apply them to your banking or insurance programme, then you probably don't need to read this book. But if you feel you have something to learn about these concepts, or you need a refresher, then stick around, I promise it will be a good investment of your time. After all, customer expectations are rising all the time, and there have never been more ways for unhappy customers to express their views to the world at large … so what are you going to do about it?

This book is not the work of your traditional futurologist, but a pragmatic approach to social media in our heavily regulated financial services industry. Please don't spend too much money on the technology, start where it makes sense, start building your social media presence now, design your content strategy, and make sure you convince people of the value of your social media initiatives and reward your community for the time your members spend visiting, commenting, contributing, and promoting them.

If you are not already, I hope by the end of this book you will be as passionate about social media as I am.

Christophe

PS: If you like this book and you feel the need to read more about social media and financial services, I'd like to point you in the direction of the following people (please note that the list is not comprehensive).

From the banking industry
Brett King – bank 2.0, customer behaviour, innovation
Peter Aceto – employee advocacy, leadership, transparency
Frank Eliason – customer service 2.0, social media
Jim Bruene – online finance, PFM, mobile
Jose Antonio Gallego – community management, social media

Matthias Kröner – investment 2.0, social media ROI, virtual currencies
Jean Philippe – leadership, transparency
Pol Navarro – innovation, multi-channel, mobile
Gerd Schenkel – digital strategy, socialmedia, customer intimacy
Boris Janek – finance 2.0
Daniel Gusev – innovation, payments
Chris Skinner – future of banking, regulation, payments
Franck La Pinta – HR 2.0, personal branding, social media
William Azaroff – co-operative banking, web engagement
Shari Storm – credit union, innovation, community
Andy Golding – building society, social media, transparency
Jesse Torres - social media, risk, advocacy
Morriss Partee – credit union, experience, online community
Pascal Spelier – innovation, B2B, online community
Charis Palmer – APAC news and innovations
Rob Findlay – customer experience 2.0
Bradley Leimer – database marketing, innovation, CRM
Dinis Guarda - investment, social media, SEO
Ron Shevlin - credit union, digital marketing, tea
Jesus Perez - trading, investment 2.0, bolsa
Jeff Pilcher – credit unions, branch of the future, PR 2.0
Michal Kisiel – electronic banking, payments

Outside the banking industry
Rod Brooks – insurance, WoM, online and offline engagement
Troy Janisch – insurance, marketing 2.0, personal comms
James Gardner – innovation, crowdsourcing
Olivier Blanchard – digital branding, social media ROI
Chris Hoyt – HR 2.0, social media, personal branding
Fred Destin – VC, startups, investment 2.0
Charlene Li – open leadership, groundswell
Jeremiah Owyang – web strategy, digital engagement

Chapter 1

Social media – understanding the opportunity and getting started

The benefits of leveraging social media go well beyond marketing.

Blogs, YouTube, Twitter and Facebook have quickly became essential tools to manage reputation, create innovation, develop new products (co-creation), support clients and deal with urgent situations in "real time".

Word of mouth (WoM) is increasingly powerful, and has spread fast, as the following examples show:

◆ Facebook Group against HSBC UK (summer 2007 - over 4,000 members within the first two months);
◆ YouTube Video against Bank of America (autumn 2009 - over 400,000 views within the first three weeks).

Why is WoM so powerful?

Statistics demonstrates that over two-thirds of people trust other people's recommendations, even from strangers, sometimes even from people who admit to not having much relevant product knowledge or experience, significantly more than your plain old marketing messages (if you doubt this last point go and check out the Amazon recommendations that are prefaced "I haven't read this book, but I think...").

How then can you manage your reputation, increase customer satisfaction and drive customer advocacy without some attention to social media?

Companies must listen to online conversations about:

◆ their products;
◆ their services;
◆ their brand;
◆ their competitors.

And then decide to engage, or not, based on a well thought-through social media strategy.

In the short term it is critical to know who your key influencers are, advocates and detractors, and to find the best way to engage with them.

Back in March 2007, at the online banking summit, during our panel on "web 2.0", (at the time the term "social media" wasn't as widely used as it is now) we insisted on the fact that nowadays an angry customer will always find a way to express their thoughts online, whether it is on your blog or on another one... Social media has increased expectations: now your customers expect you to show you listen to them, they want to be able to trust you.

In the longer term one of the key challenges companies are facing is how they can pool the social data collected on their clients and potentially make strategic decisions based on this user generated content (UGC).

The risk of not embracing or at the very least acknowledging social media is considerable, but I am still hearing the following:

10 "good" reasons not to embrace social media now

1. We have already tried!
2. UGC is too risky.
3. There is no clear ROI.
4. Limited marketing budget, limited resources, limited time... this stuff is too fluffy and doesn't generate benefits.
5. It's only good for small financial institutions and direct banks.
6. The mighty press office and L&C departments are not keen.
7. Personal branding and external blogging are threats to the company: we'll end up losing our best people.
8. Wait! Our new online channel will deliver everything... eventually, perhaps.
9. Intranet 2.0 and Enterprise Search... confidential documents can be made visible, that's too great a risk.
10. Can't we just focus on the basics: building investment portfolios, a single view of the customer, that sort of thing?

I will deal with each of these criticisms in turn... however, I would have hoped by now that the case for social media should be compelling to most financial institutions, certainly enough to overcome the traditional objection about ROI, and reputation. However for some reason it isn't, which is good, because it gives me a chance to write this book!

Following on from the list above, I also commonly face some other questions:

- ◆ Do I really need loyal customers? No one in the industry can really tell the difference between a loyal customer and one with inertia? Perhaps the brutal truth is that inertia is actually enough, particularly as legislation encourages customers to be multi-banked.
- ◆ Do people really want to join a bank's community? Surely there are better places to be?
- ◆ How can banks start building trust with social media? Even if branch staff blog, does this really create genuine transparency when so many of the other important decisions are being made elsewhere and behind closed doors?
- ◆ Can banks really have fans? What is a fan?
- ◆ There are very few conversations about our insurance company online. Shall we really bother to invest in social media at all?

And some concerns…

- ◆ Social media is not scalable!
- ◆ Am I doing this for the benefit of mobile users or internet users? How does the experience change from either medium, I'm confused! How must we provide a consistent customer experience on sites like Twitter?
- ◆ Limited resources, we won't be able to contact everybody and match their expectations.

Again, I'll deal with these throughout the book. Now that I have shared my list of what clients often tell me they are worried about (but perhaps shouldn't be), I'll share my list of what clients probably should be more concerned about (but aren't).

Here we go, in no particular order:

- What is your voice? What does it sound like?
- Do you understand the need for a well defined and phased budget process? How else can you fully understand a ROI?
- Do you have an appreciation of the nuances of different types of social media?
- Do you have criteria in place to judge the qualitative aspects of a project, do you know how to weigh up the qualitative aspects of a project versus the quantitative aspects?
- You launched an online community... Do you have an exit strategy that completely respects users and members? If you don't, it's your reputation that will be on the line
- Do you understand how to capture data from a successful social media project or campaign, or have an idea how to use that data in the long term, and what the return on this will be?
- Have you thought through your moderation process?
- Do you know who your influencers are?
- Do you know who your best contributors are within your organisation?
- What's your plan to integrate the electronic with the off-line?
- Do you recognise the importance of employees in social media?
- What's the difference between a community and a group?
- What's the correct name to give to the people who take part in your social media initiatives – Users? Customers? Members? Profit Centres? Focus Groups?
- Do you understand the spirit of social media?

OK, so what are your views on the lists above? I'll leave you to think about it for a minute.

Now before I go any further I think it would be helpful to add some definitions, so here goes (and with thanks to the community at Wikipedia, a sometimes mocked but actually rather fantastic example of what social media can achieve).

By the way, I am going to assume, although assumptions can be dangerous, that you have a basic understanding of some of the commonly used terms such as blogs, social network, tweets and so on, however, if you don't then don't worry but this could be a chance for you to visit Wikipedia…. The terms/concepts that I outline below are the ones which I find are frequently open to misinterpretation. If there's anything else that you still find less than straightforward to understand, then please e-mail me and we can discuss.

Some definitions from Wikipedia

Loyalty is faithfulness or a devotion to a person, group, or cause.

Brand loyalty, in marketing consists of a consumer's commitment to repurchase or otherwise continue using the brand and can be demonstrated by repeated buying of a product or service or other positive behaviour such as WoM advocacy.

Fan, sometimes called aficionado or supporter, is a person with a liking and enthusiasm for something.

WoM refers to oral communication and the passing of information from person to person.

And now some definitions of my own

Voice Of the Customer (**VOC**) = feedback, comments, suggestions on your products, your services, or your brand values shared by real customers online whether on social media sites or on your own online assets.

Member vs. customer = members are people who signed up to your online community or follow you on Twitter, based on a topic or passion, but they are not necessarily either immediate prospects nor clients, or interested in your brand or your products.

Rock stars = years ago, I borrowed this word from Tim Collins, SVP Experiential Marketing at Wells Fargo. Basically, the idea is to give your employees the ability to express themselves publicly and become the voice of the company. If chosen and trained well, it is a formidable way to connect with your market and with the right tone of voice and also gives your employees the opportunity to be noticed by the senior executives.

Reward = your success in social media lies in your ability to convince your target segment of the value of your social media activities, and to reward your members for the time they spend visiting, reacting, contributing, and promoting your initiatives. Reward is not necessarily financial, especially in the B2B space. You will find info and recommendations on reward strategies throughout this book.

Call to action = it is critical to build a communication platform and design a content strategy to produce appealing content which could be picked up and shared by as many people as possible. It is equally critical to identify your "call to action", know what the best destination is, and redirect your audience to the most relevant piece of information, be it a blog post, a Facebook wall post, a microsite, or a product page on your public website.

Share of voice = volume of conversations about your brand, your products and your services online. You aim to increase this volume relative to your competitors and change brand perception (volume of positive vs. negative comments).

Web 1.0 vs. Web 2.0 = when I refer to a site or an initiative being 1.0, I mean that the site is very static with no or limited sharing features, and no customer generated content and engagement with its visitors.

That's enough definitions for now! Even if you are still a sceptic and you don't believe in social media or you think it is not for your well-established brand, there are a few things I hope that you will agree that you can't afford not to do.

1. Learn about how social media best practice is emerging in your industry.
2. Listen to what people say about your product, your brand, your competitors, and your industry.
3. Increase your official presence on all the most popular social media sites to prevent brand hijacking and start building an audience (start now, it takes a lot of time and effort).

Let's step back for a second and look at one small example: your financial institution has been investing millions of dollars to sponsor a sporting event.

What if you could:

◆ Increase the impact and the visibility of this activity?
◆ Multiply your audience or traffic?
◆ Build long term relationships and real engagement with your target audience instead of generating one off activity?
◆ Effectively increase share of voice, improve natural search, and change brand perception?
◆ Achieve all of the above for a fraction of your overall budget?

You've already made a significant investment; it would be a mistake not to fully maximise its value, don't you think? Social media will help you do that. So would you really argue with me if I say this is just one example of the tremendous ROI social media has to offer?

Later in the book, I look at Standard Chartered UAE's recent sponsorship of the Dubai Marathon as a case study.

Providing you do it well, I believe social media gives you a unique opportunity not only to strengthen your existing relationships with your commercial (small businesses) and corporate customers, but also to drive advocacy, become an ambassador for the sector and eventually increase your market share.

But I accept that there are still some limitations to social media in banking, and it is not yet a cure for every single business issue that a company faces...have you heard talk of "Twitter-banking" or "Facebook-banking"? I touched on the subject briefly in my introduction. So far studies demonstrate that Facebook users don't seem too interested in having access to online banking features on this particular social network.

Twitter also has a reputation for not being that secure, so would you really be prepared today to do basic online banking requests on a micro blogging site? Vantage Credit Union believed so when they became the first financial institution to provide online banking within the Twitter interface. But in all fairness, it was much more of a "marketing coup" which gave the bank an enormous amount of media coverage in the US and globally. Not bad for a relatively small regional financial institution, don't you think?

Back in September 2010, the New-Zealand based ASB Bank attracted significant blog coverage when it launched "the 1st Virtual Branch on Facebook". It was a good experiment from the innovation-focused ASB Team, but in practice I called it "a Virtual Branch 1.0" to the extent that it was a basic one-to-one chat service available via a Facebook app. However, given the pace at which social media changes and adapts and ever better apps are created, who is to say that by the time of the second edition of this book, things won't have changed.

On 1st April 2011, and it wasn't an April fool's joke, Crédit Agricole Pyrénées Gascogne (CAMPG) launched "TooKam" a virtual bank relying heavily on social media. Under the leadership of its CEO, the charismatic and visionary Jean Philippe, the

French regional bank proved once more its status of one of the most engaging banks on social media worldwide with an active presence on blogs, Twitter, Facebook, and virtual worlds (yes, now more than ever CAMPG believes in the importance of the experience provided by the 3D internet).

Let's step back again

Social media has the potential to impact virtually every single department of the bank: from HR, to corporate branding, product development, corporate social responsibility (CSR), and all the way to marketing and customer support.

Leveraging social media is a great way to give more visibility to the existing content on your site and existing initiatives. It gives you a unique opportunity to support your efforts using a different tone of voice, and better connect not only with your clients but wider constituencies. At the same time, you will create the means for a dialogue. Customers can get back to you with their comments, their concerns and their ideas.

More and more financial institutions have realised that leveraging social media is a great way, perhaps the best way, to engage with students and young professionals and reach the attractive Generation Y market, and not just as a banking strategy, but as an HR strategy. Nowadays financial institutions have to be seen as innovative to attract talent and recruit tomorrow's leaders.

Gen Y's expectations are different from the older bank customers: they are not afraid to express themselves and voice their concerns, and they expect companies to listen to them and show they care. The good news is that they are also happy to participate in a social media contest or join a new online community as long as they find the initiative exciting, innovative, useful, and fun.

At one of the conferences that I chaired, it was pointed out to me that younger customers are neither profitable nor faithful to their bank, to which I can only answer that if budgets are tight, social media and viral marketing represent the cost-effective answer!

The main types of project

I see four main kinds of social media project:

1. Behind the Firewall (BTF)

Intranet 2.0/Enterprise 2.0/Social Business collaborative projects:
- internal wikis;
- blogs;
- internal social network, directory 2.0 and search.

2. Internet banking

Accessible by your clients only, in an authenticated environment, for instance in your secure internet banking via a platform provided by a third party or built in-house. For instance, give your customers access to your product managers or your experts, urge them to share their suggestions on your products or services, submit their customer reviews on your website (collected from a secure online form, and potentially displayed).

3. Business to Business (B2B)

Your target: any small or medium sized enterprise (SME) or entrepreneur.

Time is money for these people, and these members need to be convinced of why they should spend time on your site. But if you manage to convince them of the value of your community, like giving them more visibility online and providing excellent networking or lead generation, they will participate and you will gather new information and insights on them, their needs and expectations.

4. Business to Consumer (B2C)

Your target: anybody / mass market.

Customer Experience without Borders

This is the most challenging kind of project. It can be tricky to reward your members. You may even have to deal with malicious activities. But you can always address those challenges with the right moderation process.

Some advice before starting

Before launching your own online community, the most difficult challenging type of social media project, make sure it is the right thing to do for your organisation.

Questions you need to ask include:

◆ What do you want to achieve? I know it sounds very simple, but you would be surprised how many organisations don't consider it. This is a very basic project management concern, and it is crucial to understanding how you allocate your budget and milestones between upfront and ongoing activities.

◆ Would a plain old blog be more effective than an online community? Why do something complicated when you can achieve the same outcome with much less investment?

◆ Are the people you are targeting already using other social networks such as Facebook? If so, why would they spend time on another platform?

◆ Do we really need to reinvent the wheel? Is it is possible to leverage an existing platform? People are used to comprehensive and intuitive interfaces with the likes of Facebook or Twitter. It could be risky to offer them a far inferior service. Try to identify companies which provide a white label offer based on a tried and tested platform.

◆ What is critical? Identify and prioritise the list of key features you want to offer. Distinguish the nice to have from the must have. For instance, is it critical to provide an advanced member search feature? Later in the book, I will look at the late Join2Grow.biz, Fortis' online community for entrepreneurs.

Launching a new platform is not difficult, the real challenges are first to grow your member base and then to engage your members. You want your members to use your platform as often as possible, post some UGC, and recommend the service to their contacts.

I always urge my clients and my readers, regardless of the size of their operation, to adopt a pragmatic approach to social media: start where it makes sense and don't spend a lot of money upfront. Therefore:

- Leverage free online services like blogs;
- Tap into existing communities like Facebook or Twitter;
- Start focusing on a soft topic or initiative like Corporate Social Responsibility (CSR), charity work or sport sponsorship.

If possible white label a popular blogging or online community platform, make it as simple as possible to contribute and spread the word.

What will make you successful?

Success in social media lies in your ability to convince people there is a value in taking part in your initiative and a worthwhile REWARD for the time they spend:

- visiting,
- contributing,
- sharing, and
- promoting.

Why then do so many companies get sidetracked by technology?

Technology is for me a much lesser concern; however, what is important is that you make your content:

Customer Experience without Borders

- easy to find,
- easy to search and
- easy to share.

I always insist that the quality of the interface is not important in social media (as long as it provides all the expected basic features) so don't blow your budget on this. As a rule of thumb, I would suggest that you should allocate most of your budget to training your employees, designing and delivering a content strategy, engaging with your community management ongoing operational activity, and no more than 20% of your overall budget on a platform at least initially.

And don't spend huge amounts of money promoting your activities. If you do it right and if you manage to convince your influencers, they will be delighted to market your initiative on your behalf and for free (your CFO will be delighted to hear this I'm sure).

But most of all just keep learning and experimenting, preferably in as cost-free a way as possible!

Best practice is evolving all the time, new functionality as driven by Moore's Law and by the spirit of adventure that so many people in social media have, is emerging all the time. Look at your mobile and computer hardware from three years ago and assess your electronic habits from that time, you probably wouldn't use things like that/do things like that now, right?

So if there is a mantra to this industry it must be:

Social Media = Live and Learn.

But some of you are thinking, isn't live and learn an expensive process? Well yes it can be, but if you are managing your risk properly then it shouldn't be.

Often you can quickly identify areas for improvement, for example:

- Simplify and optimise your interface (my third term mentioning this point, so I shan't say it again);
- Identify passionate contributors among your employees, people with views to share, and get them involved;
- Produce a strong editorial line and focus on ever more valuable and relevant content, but please note that valuable and relevant doesn't always mean new and expensive – some of the most effective content has been retro material with a kitschy or humorous element;
- Identify your influencers (advocates and detractors) and start building relationships with them asap;
- Promote your initiatives on your own assets (public website, online banking...);
- Fully leverage all the key social media sites to cross-market your initiatives and your content.

And above all (and yes I know I am repeating myself here), find the best way to REWARD people for :
- visiting,
- contributing,
- sharing, and
- promoting your initiatives!

One of your initial key hurdles will be to drive adoption of your platform and reach a critical mass of users.

Again, let me reassure you: your interface won't be perfect at launch and that is not a big issue, take a step back... customers are now used to companies releasing beta versions of sites, and are used to being asked to comment on works in progress, wouldn't you agree? In fact they like being asked; Alvin Toffler's "prosumer"vision is now a reality.

So what will you do?
- You will observe how your founding members are using your platform;

- Then you will ask them to share their comments and suggestions;
- You will take those ideas into account, review them, categorise and rank them;
- Finally, you will deliver the ones which will have the biggest immediate impact.

Simple, isn't it? Forget technology, focus on people!

The myth of critical mass

Now I come to one of the big misconceptions. Social media is not just about critical mass.

Of course some mass is needed to form a network, but it is important not just to track the numbers, you need to understand the qualitative side, how engaged members are.

Unless you understand the nuances of different media, you will run the risk of irritating customers and have them lose interest in your message and of making yourself appear (whisper it softly) irrelevant. For this reason I have never advised a client to launch a blog, an online community or a virtual island for the sake of it. It would be a mistake.

First, you need to understand your business objectives and see if and how social media supports it. Once again it is critical to find the best way to understand and REWARD your members (have I said reward enough yet? OK, I'll leave it for a while, but you see its importance).

Having mentioned reward so much, I should probably outline the main methods of dispensing it, yes? Let me tell you this, if you fully understand how to reward your community, you are likely to be very successful with your social media initiatives... and if you don't, then...

There are four main ways to reward your community. You give them:

- ◆ visibility and networking,
- ◆ exclusive content,
- ◆ fun and entertainment, and
- ◆ a challenge / the opportunity to win a contest.

I'll look at each of the above in more depth throughout the book. In the meantime here's one example of what I would consider to be a compelling reward, (as taken from my blog post on 5 May 2009):

> "....A couple of hours ago, the UBank team informed me that "something exciting" was about to happen on @UBank shortly,
>
> "A little different to most banks on Twitter... we're gonna thank our followers, with a gift ;-) stay tuned...", "we're giving all our followers (who fill out a web form) a free UBank 1gb USB Flash (Aust residents, but we'll send you one)".

I look forward to receiving the USB key thanks UBank! ;)
It was a fresh and innovative way to:

1. Quickly increase their follower base.
2. Capture customer & Twitterati feedback in order to better leverage the leading micro-blogging platform.
3. Generate a lot of buzz from industry bloggers and journalists from all over the world in a cost effective way.

Congrats UBank!"

Relevant, not new and expensive content

In social media, content and context are extremely important.

As Simon Cowell says in his popular X-Factor shows, wannabe stars / leaders have to make themselves RELEVANT.

There is a general misconception as most companies think they have to constantly create new and exclusive content to be successful with online communities.

This isn't totally true, although of course companies must produce interesting, compelling and non-bland content.

However, I always advise my clients to identify older, existing content which might still be relevant.

Financial institutions are nearly always sitting on an enormous volume of excellent content that people are not aware of – you want examples of the type of thing?

- Analysis;
- Presentations;
- Videos;
- White papers;
- Reports.

My aim is not to overload this chapter of the book with case studies, but here is one that's too good not to mention.

American Express made a smart move on Facebook (http://Facebook.com/AmericanExpress) when it decided to re-use some of its iconic old commercials.

What a brilliant way to engage your community and again an example of creativity and imagination triumphing over budget.

A few words now about Twitter...

I'm coming to the end of the first chapter and I haven't said much about Twitter, one of the mediums that I love most. The next chapter deals with Twitter, but for those of you who can't wait, here are a few thoughts...

Even though it is easy to create an account on Twitter, building an engaged audience is much more difficult.

But let me insist again: you don't need to produce exclusive content to be successful, you need to reuse existing content, repackage it, and make it RELEVANT.

Financial institutions must learn how to write a tweet, otherwise their content would hardly stand out from the 50 million daily tweets (stats from June 2010), very few tweeps would pick their tweets and fewer would RT them.

Many FIs would surely come to the (wrong) conclusion that Twitter (or worse, social media) doesn't work for them.

#suchawastedopportunity

Six steps to success

Here then is my 6-step plan for social media success (and you'll be pleased to see that it doesn't contain the word reward).

- Learn
- Listen
- Participate
- Engage
- Measure
- Improve

One more time, I will insist on the importance of people over technology: from your advocates to your detractors... and don't forget your employees!

Some other issues to cover off in this opening chapter...

Other key issues

Personal branding and external blogging

These are an asset to the bank, please don't view this as a threat.

Nowadays, I believe it is critical for ambitious managers to "manage your brand", that is to increase your visibility online, your credibility and to be recognised in the industry at large. It opens up a whole new world of opportunities.

Not only it is valuable to an individual's career, but it makes them a great asset to their company. It is a win-win situation: the more visible, well-known and influential you are, the better the reputation of the organisation.

And yes, it is true: the more visible, the more likely you are to be headhunted. But I wonder why your company would see that as a risk?

At the end of the day, if a company is doing a good job of managing talent, they shouldn't be worried... or should they?

User generated content and advocacy

UGC is perceived more as a high risk activity (brand damage) than a great opportunity. But if you do it right, you can not only win back angry customers but occasionally you will even turn them into your best brand ambassadors. James Gardner, a person I respect a great deal and formerly Head of Innovation at Lloyds TSB, my former boss, comments:

"Innovation is risky, yes, but it can be managed as any other investment portfolios... and bankers are experts in risk management". Or at least they should be, right?

In the web 2.0 era, your client expectations have changed: they won't hesitate to express themselves online, and they want you to show that you listen to them and prove that you care. You need to respond to them.

Even very negative comments are useful as long as you respond and explain the reasons behind your (unpopular) decisions. You may even have to admit your mistakes. People will understand.

Honesty pays, yes it does. You will create trusted, stronger, relationships with your clients.

30

The importance of creating official social media assets...and now!

Do it now, even if you've read this chapter, aren't convinced by any of it and don't plan to be active on individual networks yet.

1. It doesn't take more than 20 minutes: register, upload your official logo, copy a (short) company description in Info, list your other social media assets.
2. It takes time to build an audience: you'd be surprised, but people will start following your page, even though it is not necessarily active. And the day you are ready to produce content (or even better, engage with the users), you will already have a decent group of people to reach out to...

You should really try and have someone with one of the following job titles in your organisation

- ◆ VP Social Media, Director of Social Media, Social Media Manager;
- ◆ SVP Experiential Marketing;
- ◆ Director of Reputation Management;
- ◆ Web 2.0 Strategist;
- ◆ Community Manager;
- ◆ Director, Customer Engagement.

Final comments

Chapter 1 is coming to an end here and I hope I have conveyed the spirit needed for using social media and creating a great customer experience.

So far we have had a lot of words and text.

In the closing part of this chapter I offer you some checklists and points for building a business case for a social media initiative should you need to put together (perhaps at short notice) some meeting agendas or even a project plan!

I also include some figures and diagrams that illustrate some of the points that have been covered.

Checklist 1

Starting out

Why should we do this?

- Social networks have had an impact on financial services. Therefore we need to take advantage of new technologies to create richer customer interactions.
- The credit crunch has changed perceptions of banking. Therefore... Limited trust, rise of WoM.
- Every financial institutions aims to increase loyalty and Net Promoter Score.
- Turn your customers into brand ambassadors with social media and customer generated content.
- New customer expectations across a number of industries. Therefore... The power has shifted.
- Limited IT and marketing budget. Therefore... we need a new approach

Strategy – towards customer advocacy

.... Where shall we start?

- Don't reinvent the wheel. Tap popular social media sites and white label a platform.
- Be different: people first. Innovate and focus on people, not technology

- Make it easy. To register, contribute, share, spread the word.
- Reward your members. Exclusive content, visibility, entertainment, contests.
- Spend wisely and identify the right success criteria.

Social Media? People First
- Internally: subject matter experts, social media champions, senior management, employees, community managers.
- Externally: contributors, detractors, advocates, clients, prospects, prominent bloggers.
- A phased approach to social media

Key Concerns and Mistakes
Concerns
- Ownership;
- Risk / L&C;
- Budget / ROI;
- Not for us.

Mistakes
- Tone of voice;
- Budget allocation;
- Value and reward;
- Just another channel.

Checklist 2
Recommendations for immediate action
Start LEARNING & listening now!
- Spend wisely & leverage limited resources
- Don't spend much on technology

- Be relevant: repackage & reuse existing content

Make it easy to
- Register;
- Contribute;
- Share; and
- Spread the word.

Reward your members with
- Exclusive content;
- Visibility;
- Fun/entertainment; and
- Contests.

Know Your Followers/Fans (KYF)
- Contributors;
- Detractors;
- Advocates;
- Clients;
- Prospects;
- Industry experts;
- Prominent bloggers.

Manage expectations and identify success criteria
- Key challenges;
- Create a trusted network;
- Reach a critical mass of users;
- Engage them, urge them to contribute and recommend your platform.

Manage and identify internal stakeholders
- Subject matter experts;
- Social media champions;
- Senior management;
- Employees;
- Community managers.

Employees = Rockstars

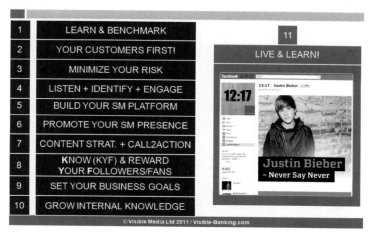

A Pragmatic Approach to Social Media (SM)

1	LEARN & BENCHMARK
2	YOUR CUSTOMERS FIRST!
3	MINIMIZE YOUR RISK
4	LISTEN + IDENTIFY + ENGAGE
5	BUILD YOUR SM PLATFORM
6	PROMOTE YOUR SM PRESENCE
7	CONTENT STRAT. + CALL2ACTION
8	KNOW (KYF) & REWARD YOUR FOLLOWERS/FANS
9	SET YOUR BUSINESS GOALS
10	GROW INTERNAL KNOWLEDGE

© Visible Media Ltd 2011 / Visible-Banking.com

Checklist 3

Tactics, challenges and concerns

Strategy

- Where shall we start? What is going on in the market?
- Tactical vs strategic;
- Senior management is reluctant (refer them to Checklist 1);
- Risk of brand damage.

ROI

- How does it fit our visible strategy?
- Where is the ROI?
- How do we measure success?

Technology

- Limited budget & IT resources;

Customer Experience without Borders

- Security / Integration;
- Vendors don't have a deep understanding of banking;
- Too many vendors / start-ups: young, size, US based, SLA;
- Procurement.

Checklist 4

The low-down on UGC

UGC and social media: the opportunity in a nutshell

- Web 2.0 projects are fairly cheap to design and roll out;
- UGC is not an issue as long as you respond;
- The challenge is to engage your members;
- Another way to reach your clients or your prospects;
- Good way to respond to new client expectations;
- Good way to convert angry clients into brand advocates;
- A chance to test new product ideas and environments, enhance customer support, recruit, encourage collaboration and foster innovation;
- Great learning experience.

Checklist 5

Some best practice organisations and projects to take a quick look at

HR & Careers: Société Générale (France), Bank of America (US)

Innovation: BBVA (Spain), Banco Sabadell (Spain), BNP Paribas (France)

Investment Management: Fidelity (US), Vanguard (US)

Facebook: ASB Bank (New Zealand), GE Money (Poland), Standard Chartered Singapore (UAE), American Express (US)

Mobile: Standard Chartered (Singapore)

Crowdsourcing: Chase Community Giving (US), Webank (Italy), Danske Bank (Denmark)

Transparency: Caja Navarra (Spain), Wonga.com (UK)

Strategy: American Express (US), Kasikornbank (Thailand), Grupo Santander (Spain)

PR: Firstdirect (UK), NAB (Australia)

Blogging: Wells Fargo (US), Rabobank (Netherlands)

Customer Service: Bank of America (US), Citi (US), ABSA Bank (South Africa)

Leadership: ING Direct (Canada), Crédit Agricole Pyrénées Gascogne (France), PEMCO (US)

Community: Amex OPEN (US), Fidor AG (Germany), Allsate (US)

Voice Of the Customer (VOC): USAA (US), GEICO (US), Capital One (US)

Checklist 6

Any Other Business? (AOB)

Social networking: Facebook or not Facebook?

What is your goal?

Why would you reinvent the wheel?

Potential solutions

- ◆ Tap into Facebook;
- ◆ Market your service in a timely fashion;
- ◆ Reward your members!

Blogging: be honest, moderate, and respond

Set up a reliable moderation process.

Dedicate resources to

- Post content;
- Monitor the blogosphere, comment bad and good posts.

Key strategies

- Strongly branded vs. discrete "powered by" logo;
- Editorial team vs. UGC;
- Blog only vs. online community.

Have you thought about Virtual Worlds?

Provide richer experiences

- Trial behind the firewall;
- 3D internet helps provide richer experience;
- Virtual worlds are becoming part of a global communication mix.

Key questions

- What is your goal;
- Who are your targeting;
- Which metaverse? – beyond second life;
- Bring your clients into these spaces.

Be an ambassador for the sector

Chapter 2
Leadership, senior executives and social media

Banking, financial services and insurance senior executives on Twitter

In a heavily regulated industry such as banking or insurance, much more than any other industry, you need the support of at least one of your senior executives to launch any kind of significant customer facing social media initiative, as proven by large financial institutions such as Wells Fargo, Citi, Bank of America, American Express, Standard Chartered, Barclays...

Indeed, you generally see more adoption of social media when a senior exec fully understands the importance of listening, engaging and reaching out to customers and employees online.

So if social media is in your remit, or you are convinced you could do a better job engaging with your clients online, then one of your primary goals is to evangelise social media in your organisation... and it starts with senior management. Like anything else, your senior executives don't necessarily have to use social media themselves to be onboard, but it always helps.

Your CEO is your best ambassador externally and your best catalyst for change internally. Using social media publicly would give more legitimacy to your internal social media effort and drive its adoption.

Here I will focus on Twitter, which I believe is one of the most convenient yet least time consuming of ways for senior execs to:

- ◆ embrace social media,
- ◆ engage publicly with their clients and their influencers,
- ◆ increase their leadership, and
- ◆ be transparent.

Peter Aceto: "I am a CEO and I tweet"

On 17 November 2010, Peter posted "I am a CEO and I tweet", where he brilliantly articulated the importance of social media, and Twitter in particular, for senior executives.

In short, Peter uses Twitter to share some inside news and drive employee advocacy – an example of leadership using social media.

I strongly recommend that you subscribe to Peter's blog and follow him on Twitter.

So, is Peter unique in the industry?

While his level of enthusiasm and his focus on leadership are pretty unique, he is not the only senior executive on Twitter. Let's look at some of the others and then return to Peter.

Methodology

Since 2010, I've started to identify Chairmen, Members of the Board, Presidents, CEOs, Managing Directors and General Managers on Twitter. I also listed a few Directors, depending on the size of their financial institutions. I used the Twitter search as well as LinkedIn's. Most of the senior executives listed have a LinkedIn account.

Due to the low number of Senior execs on Twitter, I decided not to apply a very restrictive criteria on the quality of the page (bio, avatar, and background), the level of activity, or the size of the follower base. Please note, I won't be listing CEOs of small insurance agencies (agents / brokers) nor will I list every single financial services firm (IFAs).

Quality of the accounts

You will find that the quality of the profiles, the level of activity and the size of the follower bases vary tremendously. Please find below the Top 5s (as of 24 November 2010) which will give you a better idea of the most social media savvy and active senior executives.

Top 5 oldest accounts:

1. Shari Storm @ Verity Credit Union
2. Jean Philippe at Crédit Agricole Pyrénées Gascogne
3. Gerd Schenkel (formerly) @ UBank
4. Laura Bennett @ Embrace Pet Insurance
5. Roger Grobler @ Real Insurance

Top 5 most active tweeps:

1. Rod Brookes @ PEMCO Insurance
2. Amy Leahy-McGraw @ Public Service Credit Union
3. Laura Bennett @ Embrace Pet Insurance
4. Kevin R Mullins @ The Monticello Banking Company
5. Matthias Kroener @ Fidor AG

Top 5 most followed tweeps:

1. Muhammad Yunus @ Grameen Bank
2. Peter Aceto @ ING DIRECT
3. Gerd Schenkel (formerly) @ UBank
4. Shari Storm @ Verity Credit Union
5. Alex Twigg @ UBank

The list – 48 senior executives from 14 countries

I invite you to follow my Twitter list of senior executives in banking, financial services, and insurance.

Please find below the tweeps listed by company name, in alphabetical order.

- ◆ American Family Insurance (US) - Jack Salzwedel, President
  Twitter (@AmFamJack) - Linkedin
- ◆ Banco Sabadell (Spain) - Carles Abarca, CTO
  Twitter (@carlesabarca) - Linkedin
- ◆ Barclays Bank (UK) - Shaygan Kheradpir, COO Global Retail Bank
  Twitter (@ShayganK) - Linkedin
- ◆ Barclays Bank Russia (Russia) - Nikolai Tsekhomsky, CEO
  Twitter (@Tsekhomsky) - Linkedin
- ◆ Binck (Netherlands) - Nick Bortot, Member of the Board
  Twitter (NickBortot) - linkedin

43

- China Construction Bank Asia (Hong Kong) - Terry Roberts, President & CEO
  Twitter (@tp_rock) - Linkedin
- Chubb & Son (US) - Jon Bidwell, Chief Innovation Officer
  Twitter (@joncbidwell) - Linkedin
  Articles: Innovation & SM Risk ManagementCommunity CPS Australia (Australia) - Ray O'Brien, General Manager - Distribution
  Twitter (@RazorCEO) - linkedin
- Crédit Agricole Pyrénées Gascogne (France) - Jean Philippe, CEO
  Twitter (@jcphilippe) - linkedin - blog
- Ditzo (Netherlands) - Peter Hoitinga, Algemeen directeur
  Twitter (@Hoitinga) - Linkedin
- Embrace Pet Insurance (US) - Laura Bennett, Co-Founder & CEO
  Twitter (@laurabennett) - Linkedin - blog
- Family First Credit Union (US) - Christine Peters, President & CEO
  Twitter (@ChristineP_FFCU) - Linkedin
- First National Bank (South Africa) - Michael Jordaan, CEO
  Twitter (@michaeljordaan) - Linkedin
- FIDOR BANK AG (Germany) - Matthias Kröner, Vorstand
  Twitter (@ficoba) - linkedin - blog - xing - Interview
- FORUM Credit Union (US) - Jenny Budreau, Chief Administration Officer
  Twitter (@jennybudreau) - Linkedin
- Founders Bank (US) - Jim Sturgeon, CEO
  Twitter (@JSTexBanker) - Linkedin

- Grameen Bank (Bangladesh) - Muhammad Yunus, Managing Director
  Twitter (@Yunus_Centre)
- Greenfield Savings Bank (US) - Rebecca Caplice, President & CEO
  Twitter (@rcaplice) - Linkedin - blog
- HSBC Private Bank Luxembourg S.A. (Luxembourg) - Claude Marx, Deputy CEO
  Twitter (@claudemarx) - Linkedin
- IAG New Zealand (New Zealand) - Jacki Johnson, CEO
  Twitter (@jacki_johnson) - Linkedin - blog
- ING Direct Canada (Canada) - Peter Aceto, President & CEO
  Twitter (@CEO_INGDirect) - Linkedin - blog Articles: Interview US Head of Marketing
- Metro Bank (UK) - Anthony Thomson, Chairman
  Twitter (@ATMoneySpinners)
  Articles: no social media strategy?
- Millstream Area Credit Union (US) - Karen Reams, President & CEO
  Twitter @karenreams) - Linkedin
- MiniCo Insurance Agency (US) - Michael L. Schofield, President & CEO
  Twitter (@MLSchofield) - Linkedin
- Mt. Lehman Credit Union (Canada) - Gene Blishen, General Manager
  Twitter (@Tinfoiling) - Linkedin
- NAB (Australia) - Sam Plowman, Executive, General Manager Direct Banking
  Twitter (@samplowman) - Linkedin
  Articles: Twitter + 'More Give, Less Take' campaign
- NIBC Bank (Netherlands) - Jeroen Drost, Chairman Managing Board

Customer Experience without Borders

Twitter (@JerDr) - Linkedin
- ◆ Nordnet Bank (Sweden) - Carl-Viggo Östlund, CEO (Twitter @ViggoNordnet) - Linkedin
  North Jersey Community Bank (US) - Frank Sorrentino III, Chairman & CEO
  Twitter (@FrankSIII) - Linkedin
- ◆ Novartis Federal Credit Union (US) - Ann South, President/CEO
  Twitter (@south1) - Linkedin
- ◆ Pan American Bank (US) - Jesse Torres, President & CEO
- ◆ http://Twitter.com/jstorres - Linkedin - blog
- ◆ PEMCO Insurance (US) - Rod Brooks, Chief Marketing Officer
  Twitter (@NW_Mktg_Guy) - Linkedin - blog
- ◆ Peoples Trust FCU (US) - Angela S McCathran, President & CEO
  Twitter (@amccathran) - Linkedin
- ◆ PerkStreet Financial (US) - Dan O'Malley, CEO
  Twitter (@dan_omalley) - Linkedin - blog
- ◆ Public Service Credit Union (US) - Amy Leahy-McGraw, Marketing Director
  Twitter (@PSCU_Amy) - linkedin
- ◆ Putnam Investments (US) - Robert L. Reynolds, President & CEO
  Twitter (@robertlreynolds) - linkedin - blog
- ◆ RaboDirect (Australia) - Greg McAweeney, General Manager
  Twitter (@GregMcAweeney) - Linkedin - blog
- ◆ RaboDirect (Ireland) - Roel van Veggel, General Manager
  Twitter (@Rbveggel) - Linkedin - blog
- ◆ Real Insurance (Australia) - Roger Grobler, CEO
  twitter @rogergrobler) - Linkedin
- ◆ Saffron Building Society (UK) - Andy Golding, CEO

Twitter (@Andy_Golding) - Linkedin - blog - interview
- The Monticello Banking Company (US) - Kevin R Mullins, CFO
  Twitter (@krmullins1964) - Linkedin
- TopMark FCU (US) - Angie Maynard, CEO
  Twitter (@amaynard67) - Linkedin
- Truliant Federal Credit Union (US) - Marcus Schaefer, President & CEO
  Twitter @CUschaef) - Linkedin
- Ubank (Australia) - Alex Twigg, General Manager
  Twitter @alextwigg) - Linkedin
  Articles: USB contest on Twitter, time capsule
- UBank (Australia) - Gerd Schenkel, Former Managing Director
  Twitter (@gerdschenkel) - Linkedin
  Articles: USB contest on Twitter, time capsule
- Vacationland Federal Credit Union (US) - Kevin Ralofsky, President & CEO
  Twitter (@kevinralofsky) - Linkedin
- Verity Credit Union (US) - Shari Storm, Chief Marketing Officer
  Twitter (@stormtwitter) - Linkedin - blog
- Volskbank Buhl (Germany) - Claus Preiss,
- Vorstandsvorsitzender
  Twitter (@claus_preiss - xing

...Back to Peter Aceto

Simple, transparent, honest post from Peter Aceto, President & CEO at ING Direct Canada (http://Twitter.com/CEO_INGDirect), who has brilliantly articulated the importance of social media for senior executives.

Peter is definitely one of the most active CEOs averaging 4-5 daily tweets.

Peter uses Twitter to share some inside news and drive employee advocacy.

Please find below my five favourite observations from Peter's article:

- ◆ "I can't tell you how often I am asked about why and how I actively participate in Twitter. The simple answer is this. Why not?"
- ◆ "Twitter or social media are nothing new. Twitter in particular, in its simplest form, is a dialogue and a form of engagement. That is one of the reasons why I feel my personal involvement in being transparent would be important for our brand."
- ◆ "I learned a long time ago that as a leader, you need to be authentic."
- ◆ "Yes, I'm a CEO of a bank, but I am a regular guy. My goal is to form trust, be real and accessible."
- ◆ "While social media in its simplest form is not new, the new platform of dialogue is putting pressure on organisations to commit to transparency and accessibility. Social media creates credibility and confidence but it is not a popularity contest. It requires authenticity."

TooKam.com: a social media rEvolution in (engagement) banking

TooKam.com is the latest innovative project launched by Crédit Agricole Pyrénées Gascogne, one of the 39 French regional banks in the Crédit Agricole Group, under the leadership of its CEO, Jean Philippe.

Jean is a passionate leader, and one of the greatest supporters of social media in banking. He is an active blogger and tweep which demonstrates his willingness to reach out to people wherever they are, with the right tone of voice, and lead by example at his bank.

I invite you to watch my video interview with Jean (in French).

TooKam.com (homepage)

What is TooKam?

So what is TooKam? First of all, don't underestimate the importance of this project based on its birdy name or its launch date on April Fool's Day.

TooKam is basically a(nother) virtual branch launched by a traditional bank, but with a twist. This new bank aims to be more approachable, transparent, engaging, and to give back and drive charitable behaviour.

Customer Experience without Borders

Jean is keen to prove that it is no marketing campaign but a sincere and honest try at changing the industry and making it more human and centred on the clients and those in need.

The whole project is based on an active presence on social media and the use of a virtual / social currency.

Engaging: active presence on social media

In addition to call back and web chat, the team, comprising passionate social media enthusiasts, will engage with you on Facebook, Twitter, their blog and their own virtual world.

Facebook - the TooKam.com page

The Facebook page has two main characteristics:

◆ the wall is totally open, which means that anybody can publish a post and engage with the bank, and
◆ they offer a chat embedded into the page.

As you'd expect, I had to try the chat feature on the launch date! I had a great chat with Damien who proved to be responsive and helpful.

This chat is a step forward from ASB Bank's own Facebook chat launched back in September 2010. Not only do you not need to install an application, but you can export your conversation or ask a question even outside opening hours. By the way, it is a clever way to capture email addresses.

If you are interested, I invite you to check the email export.

On the less positive side, you still don't get much background information on the agents, and I wonder how secure people will feel in this environment.

Twitter – the @TooKam_ account

For the time being, the team is using its Twitter account to re-tweet mentions of TooKam on the popular micro-blogging service, give more exposure to the blog posts covering the initiative, and invite people to interact on their Facebook page.

Unfortunately @TooKam was already taken, so make sure to follow @TooKam_.

Virtual world – the TooKam 3D branch

Jean has been convinced of the value of virtual worlds for quite some time. So it comes as no surprise to be able to interact with the team in a 3D branch.

Mobile banking – watch this space

TooKam doesn't have a dedicated mobile application just yet. For the time being, they promote Crédit Agricole's highly popular iPhone app, "Mon Budget" (My Budget).

Rewarding: Tookets, a social / virtual currency

Your success in social media lies in your ability to convince of the value of your initiatives and REWARD your members/fans/ followers for visiting, contributing, promoting your initiatives.

The cornerstone of TooKam is to leverage a virtual currency named Tookets. The bank created a standalone programme offered to charities, associations and companies to reward their members and clients and give back.

They also launched a dedicated Twitter account and Facebook page.

Basically, the more TooKam's clients are saving or using their card, the more Tookets they earn. They can then redeem those Tookets to support an association of their choice.

For the time being, TooKam provides two financial products generating Tookets:

- ◆ Saving account: you can earn up to 7,000 Tookets per year;
- ◆ Card: earn 8,000 Tookets or more per year based on your usage.

The participating associations and charities are still to be named on the site.

Social media activities in banking

Real innovation in social media is rare, but some banks have been experimenting more than the others, such as Vantage CU with their online banking service on Twitter, ASB Bank with their "virtual branch" on Facebook, or Deutsche Bank and their Q110 branch on Second Life.

52

In the last 12 months, the focus shifted towards customer support with a lot of initiatives from banks like Citi (AskCiti on Twitter, Jaime Punishill and Frank Eliason), Caja Navarra (Cancha 24), Lloyds TSB (@LloydsTSBOnline on Twitter) or BNP Paribas (@BNPPARIBAS_SAV on Twitter).

More and more banks are using social media to give to charities in a "more participative way" (or in a more practical way, as a means to increase their audience on social media sites): JP Morgan Chase with their "Chase Community Giving" initiative on Facebook (2.5 million fans), Citi with their recent Toy Story contest...

Also considering that people have been earning, buying and trading virtual currencies for years, you might wonder how innovative this initiative from "a small French regional bank" is?

The right leadership and vision

First of all, the vision and the passion are unique. Jean is committed to changing the banking industry. He aims to successfully leverage social media, with a key focus on people and proximity, to change people's perception and build an engaged community of "client advocates".

This is a typical example of a client-facing initiative which would have never happened without the influence, the conviction, and the leadership of a senior executive.

A hands-on experience

Crédit Agricole Pyrénées Gascogne has been using virtual worlds, blogs, Twitter and Facebook for quite some time now. Jean and his team are using all their hands-on experience and their passion for these channels to provide the most friendly, honest, transparent and convenient experience online.

For instance, their experience with virtual worlds reminded them how important it is to make it as simple as possible for people to join the conversation and use those new media, hence the light 3D world client and the Facebook chat.

I'm not sure how receptive the French people will be, and how willing they are to make positive contributions to the community. Success here isn't just about the number of clients or profit generated.

With this initiative, Crédit Agricole Pyrénées Gascogne has set the bar in social media and they have demonstrated that the French banking industry has become one of the online leaders.

With this experiment (led internally) the bank is a step ahead of the competition: they will dramatically increase their ability to adapt to any major future shift in communication, they connect increasingly with their market and meet higher and higher customer expectations.

Brilliant.

More than clients, raving fans

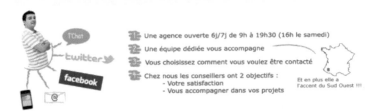

Une agence ouverte 6j/7j de 9h à 19h30 (16h le samedi)
Une équipe dédiée vous accompagne
Vous choisissez comment vous voulez être contacté
Chez nous les conseillers ont 2 objectifs :
 - Votre satisfaction
 - Vous accompagner dans vos projets
Et en plus elle a l'accent du Sud Ouest !!!

They are self-proclaimed as "the friendliest banking branch on the internet", and I truly believe they are committed to living up to this.

Everybody agrees on the fact that financial institutions are no Apple or Amazon, and they can't have raving fans, would you agree?

You know what, with this initiative I believe Jean and his team have a good shot at proving people wrong. So if like me, you are eager to find out how successful TooKam is, and how passionate, engaged, and vocal their clients will be, keep following on Visible Banking!

So still not sure what TooKam is: Is it a rEvolution? Is it a Bird? It's a rEvolution!

Chapter 3
HR, recruitment and social media

Principles

HR, recruitment and how they interact with social media is one of my favourite topics.

Indeed, in the last five years business networks like LinkedIn (globally), Xing (Germany) or viadeo (France) have revolutionised the recruitment industry.

It has given every professional the ability to market themselves, increase their visibility, and create a trusted personal brand online. Thanks to social media anyone can do it without being internet savvy.

In the last couple of years, more and more HR departments in banking, financial services and insurance have started to engage with social media channels hoping to:

◆ improve brand perception,
◆ be perceived as innovative,
◆ identify the best candidates,
◆ retain their best leaders, and
◆ stay in touch with their ex-employees.

And of course every financial institution is facing the day-in day-out challenge of recruiting better candidates, with a quicker turnaround, and lower hiring costs.

LinkedIn 1 – internal directory 0

Don't get me started on HR and knowledge management organisational failures.

You want examples?

Ok then, how about:

◆ The incomplete or out-of-date internal directory;
◆ The lack of background information on your colleagues;
◆ The inability of most companies to fully leverage the skills and previous work experience of their employees.

Do these strike you as fair points?

For instance, I've been actively using LinkedIn since 2004.

In March 2011, I was glad to find out that I was member #27, 946. I think it is the best business network out there, and a fantastic tool to identify and get in touch with the right person in pretty much every single company all over the world.

I find it a concern that I can always find ten times more information, and better and more actionable insights, on LinkedIn than on the consistently poor internal directories at some of my former employers or at some of the companies that I have been advising on social media.

Would you agree that this is a poor reflection on the general standard of knowledge management?

It is critical to build your social media expertise internally

I am a big advocate of building your social media expertise internally, and outsourcing content creation and community management as little as possible.

Indeed, as a company it is critical to make sure your workforce understands where and how to engage with your clients and meet the ever higher level of expectations from your market(s). So it is important to source social media internally; here are some of the questions I often face from clients about building a social media team.

- What are the skills required?
- Which employees could be potential candidates?
- Should I recruit externally?
- How big does the team need to be?

Scope of responsibilities

This section is designed to give an overview of resources and team structure in social media. As ever, I need to clarify a few things.

Based on my experience, even the largest financial institutions don't necessarily need a big team. They simply need to:

◆ understand where the opportunity is,
◆ find out about the best and worst practices in the industry,
◆ start listening to online conversations asap,
◆ define a content strategy (including distribution of existing content) and a response / outreach strategy, and
◆ focus on identifying their key influencers and know who their followers / fans are (KYF).

Size of the team: ownership vs. content

With social media, it is important to distinguish carefully between ownership and content.

Indeed you can give the trendy title of 'Head of Social Media' or 'Community Manager' to one of your employees whose responsibilities will include:

◆ Monitoring your online reputation;
◆ Evangelising social media internally and training your employees;
◆ Defining company guidelines;
◆ Producing your editorial line.

But beyond this it is critical to identify a *network of contributors across your organisation.*

Once your processes are in place and your contributors identified and trained, your (small) dedicated team can focus on guidance, strategy and planning.

Identifying your most social media savvy employees

1. Invite them to declare themselves on your intranet for instance, or identify the most connected on LinkedIn or the most active ones on Twitter.

2. Assess the ability and the willingness of your employees to contribute and produce some content periodically. You could start by checking out who are your most active contributors on your intranet site.

   Wells Fargo, the most experienced bank in blogging, is a great example of how to give a voice to your employees and 'turn them into rock stars'.

   And even though the bank has a dedicated social media team, led by Ed Terpening who reports to Tim Collins, SVP Experiential Marketing, the genius of Wells Fargo is to urge its employees to contribute irrespective of their place in the organisation.

3. Headhunt an expert
   You can ask a head hunter firm to find the greatest social media mind(s) to lead your social media strategy, and not necessarily from the banking industry. For instance, Citi hired Jaime Punishill and Frank Eliason, the man behind 'ComcastCares', and BBVA hired Jose Antonio Gallego from eBay.

4. Leverage your own social media assets
   You want to recruit social media savvy people, right?
   Make the job posting available only on your social media assets, and only invite social networkers to apply.

   CIMB Malaysia, who have one of the most followed pages on the Visible Banking Facebook Watch was looking to hire someone who will 'spend all day on Facebook and get paid for it'. It made sense to create a dedicated tab on their highly popular page.

Financial institutions can also use their Twitter accounts to push the job posting to their followers. As part of my Visible Banking Twitter Watch series, we are currently tracking over 30 Twitter accounts dedicated to recruitment and HR in 8 countries.

However, I would challenge the value of promoting your job postings on Twitter in an automated way without reaching out to your candidates and engaging in conversations.

Be innovative, organise a contest!

The most successful way to find your best candidates and demonstrate your commitment to social media is to organise a recurring competition. Yes, it requires a bit more time, resources and planning, but the results can be outstanding.

Since 2007, Severus Credit Union has organised an annual contest to recruit their official 'Young & Free Alberta' spokesperson.

The Breeze team at Standard Chartered announced the winner of 'the World's Coolest Intern' contest.

The campaign has been so successful (1,190 applications from 65 countries in 8 weeks) that the bank is already thinking of organising more versions in the future.

So, how did you recruit your team?

Would you consider exploring one of the more advanced options such as organising a contest?

Based on the two examples above I think it could be worthwhile.

Using career sites and traditional job boards

Well of course, you can always use the 'good old-fashioned way' of recruiting. Produce a comprehensive, very corporate job description and post it on your career site and on all the usual job boards online. After all, not every single HR group needs to be innovative, and many don't understand the potential of social media, and this is the finance industry, right? An industry that has a reputation for being a bit behind the times – ok, so this comment is a little harsh.

Having said that, if you are recruiting a lot of people, the traditional methods can still be efficient ways to fill your positions.

Banks like Citi, which is rapidly becoming one of the most engaging financial institutions in the US, and NAB, which is just starting with social media, have posted a few job openings on their career sites for respectively an Associate General Counsel Social Media Attorney and a Social Media Coordinator.

Citi regularly uses online job boards to advertise a significant number of openings.

Case studies/comments

Standard Chartered – Singapore

Aman Narain's Breeze team were looking to hire an intern to help promote the bank's new iPhone mobile banking application using social media and in particular their blog, YouTube and Twitter.

Instead of using traditional recruitment methods such as posting a job opening on the Standard Chartered website or asking a recruitment agency to search for suitable candidates, Aman decided to experiment and try something different. And after all, the new recruit would focus on social media, right?

So Aman launched "The World's Coolest Intern" competition. The results were outstanding: over 1,000 social media enthusiasts from all over the world entered the contest! As a matter of fact, the results are so overwhelming that chances are we will see more similar contests from Standard Chartered in the near future.

I wouldn't be surprised if the bank was planning to use the same approach to find a replacement to the winner, a la 'Young & Free Alberta' where Severus Credit Union invites young graduates to submit their application to become their spokesperson for 12 months. The most popular candidate (highest number of votes from the public) wins the contest.

All the contestants showed so much energy and creativity overall.

Congratulations to the winner, Katherine Liew!

She did a great job, and I must admit that for me she is the candidate who stood out the most. Katherine reached out to me via email, on Twitter, and on Facebook (a special mention to another candidate who didn't make the top 10, Audrey Ooi, who left a comprehensive comment on my post). I liked her style and her drive, and obviously I wasn't the only one.

I invite you to connect with Katherine on LinkedIn, Facebook, the 'grass is greener on the internet' blog, and of course Twitter.

Please find below a quote from Aman:

> "The number and quality of applications for the World's Coolest Intern have completely surpassed our expectations. There is a massive pool of untapped social media talent and it was definitely not easy picking our winner. Katherine wowed us with her creativity and originality showcased through a variety of social media channels. She cleared demonstrated the skills we were looking for from the winning candidate – the ability to think out of the box and engage with others, as well as the knowledge and capability with social media platforms to propel Breeze's online customer engagement to a whole new level."

Indeed, WCI not only delivered on Standard Chartered's underlying objectives such as social search (helping with SEO and optimising social media platforms), but with a softer matrix such as humanising the brand not just at community level but even at individual level.

The benefits to Standard Chartered

◆ Innovating and leading in the conservative banking industry.

◆ Generating a lot of buzz on their Breeze mobile banking suite.

◆ Free press coverage on leading online industry magazines as well as on the blogosphere.

◆ Improve brand perception not only as a bank but also as an employer.

◆ Generate traffic to the Breeze site.

◆ Improved recruitment: the bank knows more about the successful applicant, her enthusiasm, writing skills, creativity, which will almost certainly guarantee a productive and successful internship.

Benefits to the winner

◆ Working for one of the most innovative teams in the banking industry.

◆ Worldwide visibility and blog coverage.

◆ Amazing welcome: everybody at the bank not only will know Katherine (surely the CEO is aware of this initiative), but is expecting her!

Benefits to all the Participants

◆ Visibility, especially for the top 20.

◆ Great CV experience.

◆ Creates opportunities for other jobs at Standard Chartered or at any digital agencies.

Recruitment on Twitter

In this section, I will risk appearing a bit inconsistent.

I am the first to claim that it is better to have a presence on popular social media sites than not being there at all, even if you don't contribute regularly or if you just recycle content.

Social media success involves building trusted relationships with people online. You will make mistakes, and yes you will have to deal with bad comments.

But remember chapter 1, social media = live and learn. And there is a huge premium for the early adopters.

Nonetheless, companies must always make sure to constantly increase their understanding of social media and appreciate the specifics of every single channel such as Facebook, blogs or Twitter. More importantly, they must understand the expectations from different groups and types of users.

In essence, Twitter is a great tool to listen and better understand people's expectations, questions, and personal opinions in real time.

It is also an outstanding tool to share valuable insights and "blog start conversations". It takes to the next level the phenomenon blogs started seven years ago.

So anyway, here's where I might appear inconsistent...

I have nothing against the TweetmyJobs service which certainly fills a gap on the market.

It is the easiest option for recruiters to tell their management: "yes, we are on Twitter...and it doesn't require any internal resources". It is very much a tick box approach. Why not... but it is a shame to use Twitter just as another RSS feed push mechanism. Twitter has so much more to offer...

Let me share a few thoughts with you about such an automated approach.

- **Limited/no engagement:** such dedicated accounts usually follow just a handful of other accounts, and rarely engage with tweeple or join any conversation.
- **Poor content and syntax:** the syntax of those tweets are rarely optimised and the content is not appealing. Remember that people need to somehow find your tweets. Use the right hashtags and keywords, and don't abuse them in your tweets. Make your message as insightful as possible.
- **Low/no advocacy:** no engagement, poor syntax and content generally means no conversation and no RT.
- **Jobs not available anymore:** Twitter exacerbates the challenge of up-to-date information. Don't point tweeple to a page which doesn't exist or a job posting which has expired.
- **No differentiation:** I find that the frequency of updates is not great, and the Tweetmyjob bot would basically send all the updates by batch at the same time. A job seeker following the three accounts I am covering today would receive their updates pretty much at the same time, all the time.

Your Twitter account is far more than just a RSS feed: think brand advocacy.

OK, there is a value posting your jobs on Twitter, but as often as possible try to make your updates more personal and relevant. Twitter is meant to create discussions and connect people with content.

I have already commented on my automated services on Twitter which basically push job postings on a regular basis.

I must admit I am still not convinced of the value of such services.

Yes, you can claim you are on Twitter. Yes it puts your company name and your brand out there.

The key problems are the quality of the tweets (syntax), the (non) availability of the job offers, and the lack of engagement / conversations on those dedicated accounts. Twitter shouldn't been used as a mere RSS feed 2.0.

If there may be a value pushing automated tweets, they should be part of a richer content strategy. Engage more with your audience. And pay more attention to the syntax and the frequency of your tweets.

The less people notice your tweets, the less valuable your presence on this most popular of micro-blogging services.

Case studies/comments

CIBC careers

Let me illustrate my points with a few examples below from CitiJobs (no conversation, no RT) or CIBCCareers (two out of those three job postings had expired):

@CIBCCareers: CAVE Hiring Fair (Burnaby, BC) http://bit.ly/d37BjZ #cibc #cibcjobs #cibccareers #Jobs #TweetMyJOBS

Put yourself into the job seekers' mind: what are they looking for on Twitter?

Which keywords are they tracking? In the above tweet, why would you need three hashtags about CIBC? And don't forget to make your tweets RT-able!

Please note that a large company like Citi has several Twitter accounts dedicated to HR and recruitment (by the way, the HR group at Citi tends to outsource most of its Twitter accounts to an agency, which I think is a mistake).

Nevertheless, some of their other accounts are more proactive and tend to follow more tweeps, create better tweets and occasionally participate in conversations. And it shows on the stats: @

CitiGroupsJobs counts 3,500+ followers and is listed over 130 times.

Société Générale

You want to change your brand perception as an employer and differentiate yourself from the rest of your competition?

I advise you to check out Société Générale's own account dedicated to their HR brand @CareersSocGen, created by Franck La Pinta, SocGen's Brand Marketing Manager HR: Franck's approach is spot on; his team rarely advertises job opportunities, but they share valuable insights and tips for job seekers.

It is all about increasing brand advocacy and putting an emphasis on the brand values with a human tone and manual updates. More people will start connecting with some aspects of your brand they were not aware of. This approach will lead to an increase in the number of qualified job applications and the number of new recruits via Twitter.

GEICO Careers

For a fair chunk of my career, I have led new business sales teams. So this tweet from @GEICOCareers (http://Twitter.com/GEICOCareers) made me smile:

NY #Jobs: We're #hiring Sales Reps in Woodbury & Buffalo. No cold calls, base salary, bonus potential & more. http://bit.ly/GEICOApply

I love "the no cold calls". Very few people like cold calling, right? If I was looking for a sales job in insurance in NY, I would definitely consider applying! Good tweet GEICO.

Just a quick remark on the short url. Even though I like that GEICO personalised it, it directs potential job applicants to the generic job search page, I wonder how big the impact on their application rate is? At least, please provide us with the

69

job reference # like a Bank of America (http://Twitter.com/BofA_Careers).

Sunlife Careers

I would like to share with you a tweet sent by @SunLifeCareers (http://Twitter.com/SunLifeCareers): "@SunLifeCareers Sun Life Mtl #Jobs - Director, Wealth Sales - Montreal http://url4.eu/-6Jq2r"

Problem is: it directed me to a page on the financial institution's career section notifying me that the job was no longer available. Talking about managing people's expectations? At least, suggest a few similar jobs which may be of interest to me or invite me to be notified via email.

Chapter 4
Reputation, risk and moderation

So far we have looked at why organisations need to be involved in social media, the role of leadership and how best to go about recruiting a social media team.

In this chapter I look at the range of strategies and tactics connected to e-reputation, risk and moderation, including:

◆ **Listening appropriately** to online conversations about your brand, products and competitor;

◆ **Identifying** your influencers and followers and **building relationships** with them;

◆ **Designing and implementing:** a response and outreach strategy;

◆ **Establishing your social media assets:** as the go-to destination for questions and customer conversations, using rich media like videos and podcasts;

◆ **Training your staff:** creating employee guidelines (for both inside and outside office hours) and broader training plans;

◆ **Minimising risk:** implementing a robust moderation process with user guidelines;

◆ **Rewarding your users;**

◆ **Finding your voice:** identifying the right contributors, and the right tone to use;

◆ **Transparency** and **brand perception**: via social media initiatives around your brand values or CSR;

◆ **Providing excellent levels of customer support**: via proactive listening and trained support teams on Twitter and Facebook;

◆ **Empowering your customers**: capture their feedback and give them a voice – they will defend you;

◆ **Leverage user/customer generated content**: use your customer feedback to identify recurrent issues, enhance your products and services, launch new products and improve your marketing messages;

- **Going beyond the online channel**: user generated content as part of your traditional marketing (TV, press, radio);
- **Increasing overall customer satisfaction;**
- **Living and learning**: start asap, be ready to learn from your mistakes.

Will that be enough for now?

Some of the discussions that I start in this chapter will be concluded only much later in the book – I hope this is not too confusing! Let me know if I've missed something!

Key goals and challenges of e-reputation

During one recent event I shared my vision and my thoughts on the e-reputation phenomenon.

Please find below some of the key messages:

- Yes, it is important to know what's being said about your brand online.
- But your challenge *is not* to flag all the mentions of your brand, your products and services, or your competitors.
- Your real challenge is to assess the authenticity of the comments and the level of authority and expertise of those vocal people.
- You have to identify your key influencers (detractors and advocates), then design and implement a response strategy and then find the best way to build relationships with them.
- You must start building your social presence asap to be able to reach out to your customers whenever appropriate and be perceived as authentic and genuine.

Customer Experience without Borders

- You must give a voice to your customers and turn them into your best champions. They'll defend you when you need it most.

Even if every single comment was relevant and visible, I am pretty certain that you won't have the time or the resources to respond to everything. Would you agree?

Choosing (and challenging) the online monitoring solution providers

There are hundreds of solution providers knocking at your door, claiming to provide the best online reputation monitoring solution.

I invite you to challenge them not on their platform itself but on:

- Their listening capabilities on networks such as LinkedIn or Facebook;
- Their moderation process, including their range of language skills;
- Their methodology for sentiment analysis; and
- How they can help you identify your key influencers and assess accurately the level of influence of the contributors.

Try these questions on a software vendor and let me know the results ... it could be fun!

The 10-Step strategy to leverage social media as part of a reputation management strategy

10-Step Strategy to Sail Through a Crisis Thanks to social Media

1. learn the Best & Worst Practices in FS
2. Listen to Online Conversations
3. Build Relationships with Your Influencers
4. Build a Presence Where your Customers Are
5. Create a platform for Swift & Engaging Comms
6. Make Your Comms Action/Share/Search-able
7. Protect Yourself & Minimize Your Risk
8. Urge Your Customers to Express Themselves
9. Be Transparent & Authentic
10. Your Company Must Adapt: Live & Learn!

© Visible Media Ltd 2011/ Visible-Banking.com

If you want to look at each point in greater detail then I invite you to check the slides I used at a presentation in Hong Kong, as well as the links to the initiatives and best practice organisations mentioned.

1. Learn from the best and worst practices in FS

- ◆ The Visible Banking Facebook Watch Series: 720+ pages, apps tracked in 69 countries
- ◆ The Visible Banking Twitter Watch Series: 1,350+ accounts tracked in 71 countries
- ◆ @MasterCardNews
- ◆ Interview with Jim Issokson, VP Reputation Management at MasterCard Worldwide (video)

Customer Experience without Borders

2. Listen to online conversations (e-reputation)

- ◆ Google: Alerts and Blog Search, Socialmention.com
- ◆ Another Angry Customer Using Social Media: PeoplesPops' Blog Post & Tweets Against Chase Bank (Video)

3. Build relationships with your influencers

- ◆ Volume vs. Value on Twitter and Facebook: the Chase Community Giving page with 2.5 million fans and the BNP Paribas Net page with 115k+ fans

4. Build a presence where your customers are

- ◆ @bankofamerica
- ◆ GEICO's social media presence: Connect with GEICO
- ◆ ABSA Bank's Facebook page with open wall
- ◆ Lloyds TSB Supports its Customers on Twitter! Fine, but Now the UK Bank Should Learn from the Best (video)
- ◆ Wells Fargo blogs

5. Create a platform for swift & engaging comms

- ◆ South Carolina Federal Credit Union's Simple Cents blog (even COO, Troy Hall, contributes on a regular basis)
- ◆ Germany's most innovative online community bank Fidor AG's YouTube channel and their videos with their dynamic CEO (Matthias Kroener)

6. Making your comms action/share/searchable

- ◆ First direct's social media newsroom

7. Protect yourself and minimise your risk

- ◆ Open wall on Facebook: CIMB Group Malaysia and Progressive Insurance with respectively 114k+ and 21k+ fans
- ◆ Wells Fargo's community guidelines and US Bank's code of ethics

8. Urging your customers to express themselves

◆ American Express' customer reviews

◆ Standard Chartered UAE Launches 'Go The Distance' to Capture Emotional Stories

◆ USAA's customer reviews and questions and answers

◆ Crédit Agricole Pyrénées Gascogne's customer feedback on homepage

9. Being transparent and authentic

◆ Peter Aceto, President & CEO of ING Direct Canada, on Twitter@CEO_INGDIRECT

◆ The Wells Fargo – Wachovia Blog: social media can also support a banking merger

◆ ANZ staff set up fake Facebook sting

10. Your company must adapt: live and learn!

◆ First direct Twitter spam: an apology

Building an efficient crisis management strategy

Principles

My belief is that the more social media savvy and engaged your organisation, the easier it is to sail through a crisis.

Nowadays, whatever the industry, companies must empower your clients, they will become your most dedicated and vocal supporters when trouble comes.

It is also important to identify your detractors and your advocates, and start to build trusted relationships with the most influential ones.

I invite you to watch my interview with Jim Issokson, VP Reputation Management at MasterCard Worldwide shot in New York City prior to Finovate 2009.

77

It is interesting to notice that detractors are also using social media.

One example is from South Africa. I invite you to check the Standard Bank initiative started by a few angry customers in 2010. Their increasingly popular Twitter accounts and online community on Ning helped them gain some good exposure online.

Risk

Risk varies hugely across social media projects

If you can't control what people are saying on their own social media assets or social networks, you can make sure conversations on your social media assets are relevant.

But you see, there is still a lot of misconception about the risk, and for that matter, the ROI of social media.

I'd like to clarify a few points in this section.

Back in May 2009, the respected European Financial Management Association (EFMA) published in their magazine one of my articles entitled "Not embracing social media presents a new risk".

In this article, I stressed the fact that for a financial institution the risk of not embracing social media was far bigger than having a few vocal detractors online.

I also articulated what a sizable opportunity it was for the most engaging financial institutions online.

Among many other business benefits, social media gives brands a unique opportunity to:
◆ Connect with their markets;
◆ Be perceived as more genuine and authentic;
◆ Win back angry customers;
◆ Turn them into brand champions.

Crisis management and e-reputation

The types of risk in social media

First of all, we need to distinguish two types of social media activity:

1. Outside your own assets

Yes, it is important to know what is being said online about your brand, your products and your competitors. Among your key challenges are the amount of noise and the lack of information on the contributors.

No, you can't control what people are saying about you on public forums, reviews and comparison sites, Twitter and so on. You can only be aware of those conversations, and you have the option to respond. But it won't make those negative and sometime abusive or fake comments vanish.

Yes, there is a risk that an over-zealous employees decides to join one of those conversations and respond on behalf of your company.

2. Your own social media assets

This is a different issue.

Here I'm thinking of your official social media presence on sites such as:

Facebook,
Twitter,
blogging,
YouTube, and
Flickr.

As a priority, you must make sure you own your name on those popular websites (remember the closing comments from the end of chapter 1).

Three ways to reduce the overall level of risk

◆ Train your employees: put together a short question-naire, make it available on your intranet and invite all the workforce to take the test. A few best practice firms like American Family have held training sessions over lunch...

◆ Put together two sets of employee guidelines: publish on your intranet simple guidelines about how to behave and interact on social media sites both during and outside working hours.

It is important to educate your employees and make them understand the implication of engaging in potentially sensitive discussions on behalf of your brand.

Much of the time people genuinely don't appreciate the reach of social media and the potential impact of their comments on their employer's brand. Incidentally this is also true for angry customers who often regret leaving intense and angry comments online.

I strongly believe in the importance of educating your work-force and putting in place the right processes and guidelines, especially for your employees who officially contribute on social media sites on behalf of your company.

At the same time, financial institutions must remember that the level of risk is highly dependent on the type of social media activity. You must manage the risk but at the same time, you want to increase both employee and customer advocacy.

This is one of the most sensitive topics: monitoring social media activity by your employees outside work. There is no defi-nite answer, but it is growing source of concern for social media users.

As mentioned on the Socialnomics video: "what happened in Vegas stays in... Twitter, YouTube, Facebook..."

You get the idea.

November 2009, insurance company Manulife decided to cut off the allowance to a depressed 29-years old Canadian woman because she seemed happy and in good health on recently uploaded pictures on Facebook. This incident raises a huge number of issues. Do you really think insurance companies will somehow manage to increase their insurance premium up to 10% for the social media users active on sites such as Twitter or Facebook?

- ◆ **Publish a simple set of user guidelines**: publishing 'house rules' or moderation guidelines will enable you not to get rid of all the negative comments, but to possibly take offline the comments which are abusive or totally off topic.

- ◆ **Moderate your social media assets**: it is critical to put in place a process whereby someone checks your assets, especially on communities like Facebook or YouTube where the comments will be published straight away.

Implement a moderation process on your blog where the comments will be reviewed by your team before they go online.

Some financial institutions, like Progressive, are more transparent and confident than others and even let their Facebook fans post directly on their page wall.

User policies and moderation guidelines

As ever there is no point in reinventing the wheel.

There are good social media user policies available online across industries on sites such as social media governance and social media today.

I urge you to have a look at these.

But I believe the ones in our industry will be even more valuable to you and your colleagues, would you agree?

In the finance industry, employee guidelines are very rarely shared online.

Having said that, please take time to check out the comprehensive list of social media guidelines I have compiled over the last few years.

Please start now and use them as much as you can! If you already have guidelines in place then please compare them to the ones below, and if you think yours need to be added to the list then please let me know!

Facebook

- ABSA (South Africa): Disclaimer
- Barclaycard (UK): Terms and Conditions
- Barclays (UK): Volunteers - Terms and Conditions
  Articles: 100 voices to attract students
- BBVA Compass (US): Ground Rules
  Articles: Facebook promotion in the street
- Caisse d'Epargne (France): Charte de Bonne Conduite
- Charles Schwab (US): Guidelines
- Citi (US): Citi Facebook Terms & Citi
- Facebook User Content Guidelines
  Articles: Citi's Twitter strategy, Citibank US on Facebook
- Commonwealth Bank (Australia): Guidelines
- Crédit Agricole (France): Charte utilisateur
  Articles: Interview with the Managing Director of Crédit Agricole Pyrénées Gascogne
- Crédit Agricole du Nord (France): Charte, Regles, Responsabilite
- FAIRWINDS Crédit Union (US): Your Posts
- FNB Premier Banking (South Africa): Disclaimer
- Handelsbanken (Sweden): Om loggen
- HSBC Students (UK): Bursary

- Contest - Acceptable Use Policy
  Articles: video comments - Facebook contest,
  yourpointofview
- ING Direct (France): Charte Facebook
- KBank Live (Thailand): House Rules
- Kuwait Finance House (Malaysia): Important Notice
- MayStay Investments (US): Disclaimer
- Progressive (US): House Rules
  Articles: the brilliant 'Help Flo' video contest
- Saxo Bank - Sala de inversion (Spain): Aviso Legal
- SEB Sverige: Policy
- State Farm Careers (US): Community Guidelines
- Vanguard (US): Commenting guidelines

Blogging

- BforBank (France): Charte de moderation de
  commentaires
- Citi (US): new.citi.com site usage guidelines
  Articles: new.citi.com a tale of two tales
- Independent Bank (US): Community Guidelines
- Société Générale (France): Charte web
- SpareBank 1 (Norway): Blogging Rules
- Wells Fargo (US): Community Guidelines
  Articles: interview SVP Experiential Marketing, blogs,
  Facebook, Wells Fargo 2.0

Online communities

- Allstate (US): Good Hands Community - User
  Guidelines & Vehicle Vibes - About User
  Articles: virtual career fair
- Bank of America (US): Small Business Online
  Community Guidelines

Articles: comments on BofA's online community for SMEs
- ◆ American Express (US): OPEN Forum - Terms of Use Articles: Amex' online community for SMEs, Small Business Saturday, Twitter Top 10, Facebook Top 10
- ◆ Severus Credit Union (Canada): Young & Free Alberta - Blog comment Policy
- ◆ LV (UK): LV Community Guidelines

Customer reviews
- ◆ America First Credit Union (US): Posting Guidelines
- ◆ CIBC (Canada): Terms of Use
- ◆ GEICO (US): Review Guidelines
- ◆ PEMCO (US): Terms of Use
- ◆ USAA (US): USAA Moderation Guidelines

Social media
- ◆ Monroe Bank and Trust (US): Social Media Policy
- ◆ US Bank (US): Social Media Guidelines for Bank Business and Personal Use (page 39)

Monitoring online activity and influencer outreach strategy

Principles

Financial institutions have to start listening and monitoring online discussions about their brand, their products, their competitors and their industry. Then, they will have to assess the level of influence of the contributors in order to create an appropriate response.

The ultimate would be to achieve the level of social media best practice achieved by Dell which actively listens and makes sure to respond to pretty much every comment (both good and bad) about their brand online.

Very few financial companies that I am aware of have designed and implemented a proper outreach strategy. As ever, I am willing to stand corrected, so if you have created an influencer outreach strategy that deserves a place on Visible Banking – then let me know!

However, some companies are worth mentioning.

Bank of America and Wells Fargo are doing a great job on Twitter, and Citi plans to implement a thorough, industry leading, outreach strategy before the end of the year.

Stay tuned.

Moderation Guidelines

Principles

I can only re-emphasise the importance of being transparent in social media.

There will always be unhappy customers and increasingly these customers have "voice". Henceforth, these dissatisfied customers have the opportunity to speak louder than before on established communities.

Financial institutions that are more cautious tend to view user-generated content as "uncontrollable" and a major risk to their reputation. Another view is that banks have a unique opportunity to identify those comments in "real time" and respond quickly. It is this ability to listen and reach out on social media that enables companies to retain disappointed customers and turn them into true champions of the brand (and in turn improve their products or processes).

Know that in most cases, you will not even join in the conversation; it's your community who will be responsible for answering very negative and often inaccurate comments.

You want to allow your members or your fans to express themselves freely and react to your articles and other news.

It is important to encourage this exchange, while being transparent.

Each brand has a different approach to moderation.

For example, Progressive Insurance in the US. will leave almost all of the comments, including those that appear aggressive, so be sure to clearly display your "charter user" and your policy of moderation.

Unlike a blog, moderation on YouTube or Facebook is made "ex post".

It should not create too many problems from the moment you set a robust process of monitoring your wall. You have to find the right frequency. My suggestion is that you visit your page at least three or four times a day.

Progressive Insurance

The Progressive Insurance team does a great job of listening to conversations involving their brand, on social media sites. Progressive is very open-minded and allows Facebook users to post on their wall, even extremely negative messages.

They believe in transparency, and contrary to most they really go for it.

So, how does your moderation strategy compare?

Chapter 5
Innovation: crowdsourcing, Labs and Foursquare

Case studies/comments

The WePad Project by Webank

The WePad project: 6 weeks, 6 experts, 1 application
Italy's Webank is giving innovation a good go.

In late January 2011, they launched the WePad project, where the invited six experts and the general public help them create in six weeks the best iPad application for banking.

This is genuinely the next generation of crowdsourcing in banking. The bank recognises that innovation doesn't necessarily come from within the bank.

I remember meeting with Webank's Vittoria La Porta, PR & Brand Reputation Manager at the Online Financial Services in Athens in November 2008. At the time, Webank's social media activity was very limited. In the last couple of years, they became the most engaged bank online in Italy with a Facebook page, a Twitter account, as well as initiatives such as online dial 1999.

How the project works
A web reality and a race against time. A social network and an experiment in collective creativity. A team of experts working on an impossible mission: to make the iPad app more useful than ever, that saves time and money.

Webank holds a weekly brainstorming session during which the experts share their progress and discuss the new ideas from them or the online crowd.

The first brainstorming session with the experts took place on 2nd February 2011.

I like the fact that the weekly Top 5 most commented topics or features submitted by the community are clearly listed on the WePad website. The ones for this first session were:

◆ App for all accounts;
◆ Tag my reality;

- ◆ Not only wishes;
- ◆ iTransition;
- ◆ App for taking notes.

The 7th team member: you!

We all know that the more engaged in product co-creation your market, the more successful your new products. As ever to drive the volume of contribution the bank has to convince web users of the value of taking part. Webank decided to give away one iPad to the best contributor.

Promotion: homepage and social media assets?

Webank does a good job promoting the WePad project on:
- ◆ Its public website (dedicated tile on its homepage);
- ◆ Its Facebook page (dedicated tab which redirects to the microsite, and wall posts on mobile banking and iPhone / iPad);
- ◆ Its Twitter account (the call to action could be improved, but most of their tweets in February are referred to this initiative).

My take

Well done to the team behind this initiative at Webank.

This is one of the far too rare explorations in the field of crowdsourcing in banking; it pushes the boundaries in a fairly conservative industry.

Unarguably, Webank reaffirms its commitment to being the most innovative and engaging bank in Italy.

Such an approach is an excellent way to build a community of passionate, vocal, and influential supporters who would surely be happy to contribute to any future similar initiatives.

Here, Webank has a unique opportunity to build an engaged community of enthusiasts.

As usual, the challenge is to make sure the contributors are representative of their target segment and are rewarded for their contribution.

I'd love to find out:

◆ How many of those contributors are already banking with Webank?

◆ How influential those contributors are?

◆ If this initiative could impact the propensity of non-customers to switch to Webank... ?

Contrary to other innovative initiatives such as ASB Bank's Virtual Branch on Facebook (the New Zealand bank experienced tremendous online coverage last year), I haven't noticed either a sizable blog or press coverage online yet, or a high number of enthusiastic conversations on Twitter. I'm not sure how structured Webank is in terms of reputation management. I would recommend they find some inspiration from companies like MasterCard (I invite you to watch my interview with my friend Jim Issokson, VP Reputation Management at MC Worldwide whose responsibilities include identifying and building relationships with their influencers – journalists and bloggers). This is one efficient way to spread the news and accelerate WoM.

I'm also curious to see what will materialise from this initiative, and how quickly the bank will release its ground-breaking iPad application. With so many iPad applications dedicated to banking already available worldwide, I wonder how much better this one will be (could be?) in terms of design and functionalities.

This excellent initiative would have been totally awesome if launched 6-12 months ago, don't you think?

Idebank by Danske Bank

In February 2011 I caught up with Thomas Heilskov, manager, group online communications at Danske Bank. Thomas made me aware of Danske Bank's latest initiative in the social media space: Danske Idebank on Facebook.

I invite you to watch the interview I shot with Thomas a couple of months ago about Danske Bank's social media strategy.

Danske Idebank: improving the bank's mobile banking solution

Once more, Danske Bank demonstrates its commitment to be a better bank, more engaging and more transparent. In this case, the Danish bank wants to improve its mobile banking solution based on their customer feedback.

Please note that the initiative was time limited; Facebook users had until mid-March to submit their ideas and suggestions.

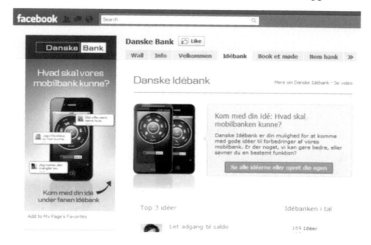

Here is more info on Danske Bank's mobile banking offering (source: YouTube):

> "With Danske Bank's Mobile Banking application, you can keep track of the economy with a single click on your iPhone, iPod Touch, or iPad. For example, you can check your

accounts, transfer money and convert amounts to more than 25 currencies. The application can also help you find the nearest ATM, branch and contact us."

Here is below an extract of the Terms & Conditions of Idebank:

"Danske Idebank is developed by Danish Bank A/S and found on the Danish Bank A/S's Facebook page. The purpose of idea bank is to get input and ideas for improvements and / or new products and services from anyone who may have something to say."

A Facebook only initiative: tab, application, blog, videos

I love that the bank identified Facebook as the best vehicle for this initiative.

It includes a dedicated tab "Danske Idebank" and Facebook application "Idebank" including a blog and a few videos.

The blog section contains just a few posts so far, all written by Esben Torpe Jørgensen, Consultant - Online Channels at Danske Bank Group.

Structured data and interactive display

Two of the key challenges of social media and UGC are getting rid of "the noise", the vast amount of unstructured data, and identity who the contributors really are.

Danske Bank has invited users to submit their ideas using one of the four available categories:

◆ Features (136);
◆ Design (14);
◆ Information (33);
◆ Other (20).

The bank did a good job with only 20 ideas in the "Other" section.

Equally critical for a user is the ability to find the relevant piece of information and display the result in an easy, interactive and relevant way. Here the bank gives four options to sort the ideas already submitted:

- ◆ Most popular;
- ◆ Most commented;
- ◆ Most recent;
- ◆ Ideas from my friends (my favourite option!).

Activity and usage

In its first few weeks, Idebank generated a good level of activity and usage. It is a experiment which already generated a good level of involvement.

Here are a few stats:

- ◆ 9,950+ monthly active users;
- ◆ 2,000+ votes;
- ◆ 169 ideas;
- ◆ 128 comments.

Urging Facebook users to contribute and share their ideas

The best element of this initiative is that Danske Bank gives the power to its customers and offers a platform to share their thoughts and opinions in a very open way.

Again, from About and Terms & Conditions:

> "Come with your idea: What could a mobile bank do? Danske Idebank is your opportunity to come up with good ideas for improvements to our mobile banking. Is there anything we can do better, or if you miss a certain function?"

Here, the REWARD for the contributors consists essentially of:

- ◆ getting some visibility on the Danske Bank Facebook page (for the top 3 contributors, left handside), and
- ◆ getting to influence product development.

93

Top 3 ideas so far:
- Easy access to balance;
- Registration for PBS;
- GPS tagging of my expenses.

Questions to the top contributor

I'd like to focus on the contributor with the top rated idea so far, Jacob Høffer Larsen. I contacted Jacob who discussed Idebank.

- *How did you hear about Idebank?* I heard about it from "offline" friends, but also there have been banners on Facebook and in the newspapers. Also I can see that friends on Facebook are using Idebank.
- *Are you a Danske Bank customer?* Yes I have been a customer my entire life.
- *Would such an initiative increase your propensity to become a client or recommend the bank to your friends?* The Idebank is about new ideas for the mobile app, which I'm very satisfied with. That app would be a reason for me to recommend the bank to my friends. Also I think that Idebank makes Danske Bank look more transparent and honest. Instead of making nonsense push marketing, they here connect with me in a more intelligent way. This means that the balance of power between them and me is more equal. I get the feeling that I help them, and humans like to help other, so I get a positive feeling about Danske Bank. I feel that they listen and are innovative.
- *What do you think of the Facebook application?* I think the Facebook application is very professional and has a good user interface.
- *What compelled you to take part and spend time sharing your ideas on the platform?* The reason I participated with an Idea is that I'm very pleased with the mobile app that Danske Bank has, and therefore have a positive feeling

about Danske Bank. Also I think it is a very good idea to involve the users in innovation generally, so I wanted to take part. I also have a competitive feeling about it, and wanted to see if I could come up with a good idea that others would like.

◆ *How happy are you to do that on Facebook?* I'm happy to do this on Facebook because I'm used to Facebook. Some people might not see Facebook as a serious platform for a bank, but I think it is a good thing to meet the customers in their natural surroundings.

◆ *Any suggestions to improve the interface / initiative?* I think it would be even better if Danske Bank also commented on the ideas. They could tell us if the ideas are possible from their view. The might do that when the time has ran out - if not it is a big mistake and the project might lose some of its credibility!

Big thanks again to Jacob for taking the time to contribute.

Jacob (@jhlarsen on Twitter) is currently writing his master thesis on "How to implement crowdsourcing/open innovation" with Socialsquare.dk.

My take

Leveraging social media, in this case Facebook, should be essentially about engaging with your community and sustaining meaningful conversations with your members, not just launching a short term PR 2.0 campaign "a la NAB's the Break Up" with limited interaction with your customers, or limited relationship to your brand "a la BNP Paribas Net on Facebook" where the French bank essentially gives away cinema tickets on one of its main official page.

Danske Bank has chosen one of the best ways to leverage its page: mobile banking is still cool and innovative, and customers are enthusiastic. The feedback is not a concern because it doesn't involve products, and it gives the bank a unique opportunity to identify its key advocates, the most passionate and influential customers about mobile and innovation, and build relationships with them.

This is an excellent experiment, just like ASB Bank's Virtual Branch on Facebook or Webank's crowdsourcing Wepad Project. I can't wait to find out more about the insights from these three innovative initiatives.

Even though the Danish bank has generated a good volume of activity, it has also experienced two key challenges which limited its success:

♦ **too much visibility for the early contributors** which made it difficult for new contributors to join the top 3;

♦ **the lack of proper REWARD** which impacted upon the propensity of the contributors to spread the word around them and urge their contacts to participate.

As usual, the more visibility you give to the idea the more votes they'll get. There is a clear advantage to be one of the first contributors. It happens often, for instance assess the Standard Chartered UAE "Go the Distance" story campaign, or Bank of America's small business online community.

I can't wait to see how the bank will leverage this input, how quickly they will implement some of the best recommendations, and explain why they can't implement some of their favourite ideas (after all, the bank has its limitations too).

Also, once the initiative is closed I wonder what will happen to the tab? Will the tab disappear like Citibank US's Holiday tab which also contained user content? Will the bank redesign the tab to focus on the key results as Chase Community Giving did with their "Chase Giving" tab?

I'd love to see them using the same approach to gathering customer feedback on a financial product or a service such as online banking or e-statements.

Update – Idebank Phase 2 (May 2011)

On 12 May, Danske Bank launched the second edition of its innovative Idebank crowdsourcing initiative on facebook which will run for 4 weeks. The concept was validated following the success of the first edition back in March 2011 (just covered previously in this book).

A More Serious Topic This Time Around

It was smart to start this experiment with a topic people love and which is not purely a financial product. Mobile Banking was perfect, and to convince yourself you just have to check the excellent stats enjoyed by Danske Bank at the end of the 1st edition: 263 ideas, 185 comments and 3109 votes. During the intiiative, the bank also dramatically increased the size of their fan base.

This time the topic of interest is "Housing and Mortgages", not quite as sexy as "mobile banking" is it?

This is a great second step from Thomas Heilskov, Manager Group Online Communications, and his colleagues. Indeed banks have to start leveraging social media to talk about "serious topics" like financial products and involving their customers more in their product / service creation and enhancement processes.

The team don't expect a high number of ideas or comments, and it makes total sense. But not only don't you necessarily need hundreds of non-actionable ideas but a few good ones, it also demonstrates your willingness as a financial institution to be transparent and to listen.

It is a great way to support their current projects with access to more relevant and fresh customer input, and validate the value of their decisions and their current activities.

Foursquare – Caja Mediterraneo(CAM)

In the last two years the Spanish banking industry as a whole has been one the most active in the social media space worldwide:

from the leading global banks like BBVA, domestic banks like Banco Sabadell, or regional saving banks like Caja Navarra or Caja Madrid.

Let's focus on the saving banks here, the 'Cajas':

> "In Spain, savings banks or cajas are private financial institutions organised as foundations. When they were first created, their main identifying features were their concern for saving, focus on the poorer classes, concentration in a geographical area, and allocation of a significant part of their profits to social and charity projects." (source: Wikipedia)

Spanish cajas are legally obliged to take part in social activities and charitable work. Most of them quickly understood the importance and the value in leveraging social media to give more visibility to their initiatives and build long term customer relationships.

Caja Navarra achieved worldwide fame when they launched their Civic Banking strategy based on transparency and customer engagement. Caja Madrid is very active online with their Obra Social communities.

Caja Mediterraneo taps into foursquare to increase and reward visits

In December 2010 Gerardo Prieto, Community Manager at Caja Mediterráneo, contacted me to inform me of their recent initiative on foursquare.

Basically the bank aims to drive the number and frequency of visits to their social centres by rewarding the most frequent visitors, and foursquare users, for those visits.

At this stage, the bank invites people to check in at about 20 locations in 10 cities along the beautiful Costa Blanca. Do you know that part of Spain? I strongly recommend Moraira and its surroundings!

Locations are: Caja Mediterraneo's classrooms, exhibition halls, libraries and CEMACAM, Centres Mediterranean Environment Fund.

If you are the most successful location at the end of the month, the bank will give you a prize which could be books, tickets or DVDs.

On January 3rd, Caja Mediterraneo announced the first 8 winners on its blog. In addition to giving them some kind of prize, the bank gave them visibility in the form of a link to their foursquare profile.

Those first winners got a copy of the second edition of 'The Spanish Phantom', a book for charity costing €18 which will help fund the project 'The Value of Children' of the NGO Save the Children.

I couldn't find much promotion of this initiative on CAM's online assets, apart from their blog posts and the occasional tweet on @CAM.

By the way, I invite you to check Caja Mediterraneo's social media presence on Facebook, Twitter, YouTube.

Comments

This is a good move from CAM.

It doesn't take much resource at all and they became one of the very first banks to adopt such a mobile location based approach to CSR.

You would expect some positive buzz online and some good local and potentially international, press and blog coverage.

The approach based on social media and charity is spot on! I believe it's going to be challenging to urge banking clients to come to their branch more often: why would people do that?

If popular, does a bank really want to increase the waiting time in their branch network? Success would lie in your ability to somehow target branches with a low volume of visits, and find a compelling reward.

Here we are not talking about banking or financial products, but doing something useful for the community and helping people. So in this case, maybe the reward is not so important Most of the 20-something locations don't have any more than a couple of check-ins which could explain the limited take-up of foursquare on the Spanish east coast, and the limited promotion from the bank.

The next step for CAM is to promote this innovative initiative more, if not on their website, internet banking, mails and emails to their clients, at least on all their social media assets.

I suggest they upload a short video on their YouTube channel, send more frequent updates on Twitter, and create a dedicated tab on their Facebook page and post on their wall more often.

Thailand's Kasikornbank launches "the Debit Card Foursquare Limited Edition"

The Debit Card Foursquare Limited Edition

Kasikornbank's social media activity doesn't rely solely on Facebook or Twitter. The bank is now trying to leverage mobile and geo-localisation to drive traffic to their branches and REWARD their customers in visiting them. And they do it in style.

The bank has tapped into the popular foursquare service in an innovative way and I believe became the very first bank to launch a dedicated debit card offer.

Chapter 5: Innovation: crowdsourcing, Labs and Foursquare

Please note that the KBank Live team has its own foursquare account.

In the last 18 months several banks and insurance companies in the US and in Europe tested ways to leverage foursquare, usually with limited success.

Promotional offer on KBank Live's Facebook page

The KBank Live team created a dedicated "foursquare" tab on their popular Facebook page. This tab is static and merely displays a picture about the initiative.

I invite you to find more information on another "landing page" on Facebook (the KBank Live shared this link directly on their wall).

My take

I love gateways between the real world and online, so congrats to the KBank Live team for the launch of this promotional offer and the debit card!

I can't wait to find out how the active audience and engaged dialogues on Facebook will help Kasikornbank drive a sizable volume of regular check-ins, and demonstrate an impactful and valuable use of foursquare in banking. And more importantly, how appealing will Thai people find the REWARD?

In case of an incredible success, I wonder how the branches would deal with the high volume of visits/check-ins? Ideally, the bank will offer foursquare users a personalised welcome, but how would their other customers react to that preferred treatment?

Online innovation and social media from the Spanish Financial Institutions

Since the launch of their Civic Banking concept back in 2004, Caja Navarra has been the most passionate champion for transparency in banking, constantly innovating and embracing social media to give a voice to their community.

Check out their community blogs.

In the last 18 months, BBVA has been one of the busiest banks in social media: they launched their own online community, actibva.com, and they engage with their clients via their personal financial management service/community provided by money-Strands Tucuentas (You count); they launched their virtual campus to attract talent, and demonstrate their commitment to innovate on their planta29 blog.

And even though nothing major has materialised yet from the Banco Sabadell Labs, launched by Banco Sabadell in partnership with IBM, stay tuned! Indeed, head of innovation Pol Navarro is one of the most enthusiastic champions for social media and understands it well.

The Bankinter Labs

And in November 2010, Bankinter launched their Bankinter Labs.

It is not their first initiative in the social media space, back in October 2007 the bank opened a branch in whyville.com, a learning-based virtual world for digital kids.

Interviews @ BarCampBank in Madrid

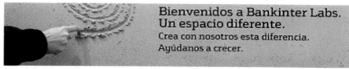

Bienvenidos a Bankinter Labs.
Un espacio diferente.
Crea con nosotros esta diferencia.
Ayúdanos a crecer.

Bankinter Labs aims to share the ideas we are working in Bankinter to receive your opinion on how we can improve and give better service.

To achieve this, we provide the tools necessary to encourage your participation and collaboration in each project. Bankinter Labs is based in the community, without you this is nonsense. Our commitment is to innovate, create and listen to your measure.

Every day, the Bankinter Labs team is working to launch new projects; our basic motivation is to be part of one of the most innovative web 2.0 projects. We firmly believe that this laboratory will not be one more, we show what we do, the projects we develop, always with the level of demand that those who trust us plant in us. Welcome to Bankinter Labs A different space. Create with us this difference. Help us to grow.

Source: about us page via Google Translate

Perfect approach to promote innovation

I love Bankinter's initiative based on no nonsense / no frills, a very simple yet ok interface... and a presence on the most popular social media sites to increase awareness and drive contribution in a cost effective way!

Releasing such a platform doesn't take too much time or money. In the current climate, where most financial institutions have slashed their innovation budget or simply shut down the innovation function, this is the right approach.

Kudos to the Bankinter Innovation Team!

Chapter 6
Becoming an ambassador for a market

The power of stories

Principles

In this section, I look more broadly at the connection between customers, emotions and (brand) values.

Capturing stories in CSR, sport sponsorship or charity work is an excellent, virtually "risk free", approach for financial institutions to improve brand perception through social media.

In the coming years, capturing customers will be one of the biggest areas of marketing in financial services.

Let your customers do the talking, and invite them not to talk about products like a loan or a credit card, but what they did with the money and how it changed their lives one (insert preferred unit of currency) at a time.

Smartypig is one great example of goal oriented savings.

People are not especially good at saving money, but we all have life events to finance.

People who set up specific goals and communicated them to their family and friends are more focused and committed. You asked for contribution so you can't really give up, can you?

If implemented well, a social media programme including customer reviews or stories gives a financial institution a fantastic opportunity to improve:

◆ Brand perception;
◆ Natural search and a variety of conversion rates;
◆ Increase share of voice.

At last! I sense you are thinking it is social media with a measurable ROI.

But it is not as easy as it seems. You have to:

◆ Design and implement a data capture strategy;
◆ Implement a robust moderation process;

- Distribute the stories on as many relevant channels as possible, including your website, your Facebook page, your Twitter account, even your offline marketing.

There is the need for a truly integrated impact beyond online. Standard Chartered is one of the best known banks to have launched a campaign about stories, and I will come to their story shortly.

In the meantime please find below comment on four other banking initiatives.

- **Citi (2010):** I invite you to visit the Citibank US page on Facebook and check their 'toy story' campaign. So far, they've collected 160+ stories.

- **Frost Bank (2010):** This bank in Texas started to collect stories and display them on the 'What Frost Believes' microsite. Frost regrouped their customer contribution in 11 "principles" (categories).

- **USAA (2010):** the most innovative financial institution in the US has started to capture member stories. They are already displaying over 240 stories on their public website.

- **Wells Fargo (2008):** between May-July 2008, WF launched a social media campaign, Someday Stories, to urge their clients to describe their "true, aspirational story about you, your family members or your friends that identifies a financial need that Wells Fargo has the ability to help meet".

In all of these cases companies are generating discussions far removed from just financial products, but on how they have impacted on people. Please note that the banks are not even talking, writing copy or doing 'conventional marketing' but are giving customers a platform to express themselves.

I invite you to read an excellent post on the Bazaarvoice blog by Heather Sassone, Client Success Director: 'Three ways customer stories can enrich your social media strategy'.

Heather articulates extremely well the importance of having a highly trained moderation team and how implementing stories as part of your social media programme creates a huge boost for your business.

Stories really can:

1. Associate your brand with themes customers are excited and passionate about.
2. Add a human dimension to your products.
3. Engage fans in the conversational context of social networks.

Standard Chartered UAE – go the distance

Comments

I think SC UAE has made another smart move.

They are still experimenting, yet they've already achieved a lot on Facebook and developed a good understanding of the rules of engagement on the popular social network.

Dubai's Marathon is the event the bank is targeting as part of this initiative, but SC as a company is sponsoring eight other marathons so you imagine the potential if this can be successfully rolled out.

People are usually passionate and proud to be running a marathon, whether it is a one-off to prove something or raise money for a good cause, or part of your life like the professionals or semi pros whose aim is to get as close as possible to the mythical 3h mark (for anyone who doubts how intellectually involved and passionate runners are I point them in the direction of Haruki Marukami's excellent What I Talk About When I Talk About Running, this can be your next book to read after you have finished this one!)

Runners are vocal too, they share tips and they invite their friends and contacts to support them.

So if you give them the ability to express themselves and add a reward to it, they will surely participate, and there will be buzz. I think it is a great initiative which could easily be scaled up and rolled out all over the world.

I am eager to find out how many stories the bank will collect and how many positive conversations the initiative will generate.

Content and contact collection

I wonder which content collection mechanism SC UAE have used?

Have they designed an email campaign to reach out to their clients, the previous Dubai Marathon runners, the aspiring Dubai Marathon 2011 runners, or the local running groups?

By experience, the email response rate for stories is significantly higher than the industry average for email marketing.

When I last looked, 44 stories were live on the microsite. I appreciate SC UAE has just launched the campaign, but considering the great visibility given by the bank on its online assets, and how simple and fast it is to register and submit a story, I was expecting a little bit more.

Please note that:

a) I may be a bit too enthusiastic here;

b) For what we know the bank may have received hundreds of entries awaiting moderation.

The registration process gives SC UAE an excellent opportunity to gather email addresses.

My key question to the bank is how they do plan to leverage those email addresses and those contacts after the marathon?

Where will they display the key stories?

Display

I'm not sure why but so far I've never been able to display the story captions, which is a bit disappointing considering a few words bring context to a picture, and stories need words, right? This issue plus the way stories are currently displayed may minimise the impact on SEO and natural search.

Contributors and reward

Great to see that SC UAE made it easy to:

◆ register,

◆ submit a story, and

◆ participate.

But as usual, I can't help but wonder if the less social media savvy runners' chance to actually win an iPhone is actually pretty slim.

I observed this during the highly visible 'Chase Community Giving' campaign on Facebook which in 2010 attracted over 2.5 million Facebook users. The more online / offline promotion the charity did, the more mobilised their fans, the more visible online, hence the more chances of making the Top 200.

Some suggestions for improvement...

To increase the chances of the newest entries, I would give more exposure to at least three or four random stories and improve the browsing experience by introducing categories.

Social media integration: Facebook and Twitter

Now, let's talk about social media integration and in particular Facebook and Twitter!

Sorry to disappoint you (I know I was), but there is no proper Facebook integration or application available.

The dedicated tab on SC UAE's main corporate page only redirects to the microsite. To stay in touch, you are invited to like the page, which means that the bank will surely increase its follower base but it will impact its quality, would you agree?

I'm curious to find out how the bank plans to communicate to those new fans that are simply interested in running?

They are not likely to be thrilled with updates about the bank or their future contests. Or am I wrong?

On the other hand, I really like their wall updates and their tweets mentioning the reason for running the marathon: they are catchy and make me want to click, see the picture and engage more.

Well done.

It's a shame the bank in UAE hasn't created a dedicated hash tag to cover the campaign, like @StanChartBreeze's #wci used in Singapore to cover their 'the World's Coolest Intern' campaign on Twitter.

Impact, goals and challenges

It's great for the bank to experiment and roll out an initiative like this.

They'll gather some excellent insights and they'll be able to confidently focus on customers next. The bank will also face key challenges including content collection and moderation.

I wonder who is helping SC UAE with the moderation process?

Moderation is easily the most demanding and rigorous process in a social media programme, although often the most undervalued.

From personal experience I know that, even the digital agencies are reluctant to provide this critical bit. Indeed, it is time consuming and it requires a large, highly trained, sometime multilingual, workforce.

Conclusion

If executed well, the campaign should:

- ◆ Deliver for the brand (awareness and perception);
- ◆ Impact the size (and the quality) of their fan base on Facebook;

- ◆ Help the bank to fully maximise its investment in the Dubai Marathon (and in the future the eight other marathons).

However, with the current setup the bank is unlikely to experience a big surge in SEO.

Citi – childhood's toy stories

Comments

Similar to Chase bank with the 'Chase Commmunity Giving' page, Citi also engages with charity, but this time not only to drive awareness of its page and create online buzz, but also to drive content creation and activity.

It is a give-give (win-win?) situation, right?

You produce content for Citi (which nicely supports the bank's content strategy on Facebook, its blog, and also on Twitter); the bank in turn will give money to the 'Toys for Tots' charity.

In contrast to Chase Community Giving where you could promote a charity of your choice, here you don't have any option. How would you compare and contrast these approaches?

Even though the topic of childhood toys is:

- ◆ Cute (people get sentimental thinking about their childhood),
- ◆ Current (the immensely popular 'Toy Story 3' is based on old toys from the past),
- ◆ Seasonal (the campaign was started in the run up to Christmas).

I wonder how appealing this incentive will be to Americans?

And 10,000 stories seems like a huge number in order to raise $100,000, don't you think?

Once the 10,000 stories are collected, how will Citi will make the most of all this user-generated content? Will they include some of the most touching stories in a future traditional or digital marketing campaign?

Chapter 6: Becoming an ambassador for a market

Turning your clients into loyal brand ambassadors: voice of the customer and transparency

Capturing the voice of the customer

Capturing and leveraging "the Voice of the Customer" (VOC) is a big challenge, it is also increasingly critical and a tremendous driver for differentiation.

We can distinguish two key approaches to VOC projects: reactive and proactive. The latter offers the biggest opportunity to change brand perception and increase market share, if you are successful.

Be reactive like everybody else

Virtually every single financial institution I've met in 2010-11 is looking for an online conversation monitoring solution. eReputation is fashionable, even in banking and insurance.

Noise

If it is important to listen, and be aware of online conversations on your brand, your products and services, and your industry, monitoring what is being said on the web presents a few major challenges such as dealing with the high volume of content, the significant level of noise, and the debatable authenticity of the contributors.

Contributors

From my experience, financial institutions have limited resources in this area, so it is critical to identify the most important conversations and comments. And if it is relatively easy to keep track of the number of occurrences; it is more difficult to assess their real level of influence and importance. And who are those contributors? Are they real clients or competitors? Perhaps it's just consultants or personal finance gurus?

Response

Afterwards, you need to design and implement a response strategy, and ideally an outreach strategy whereby you, as an organisation, officially join the conversation outside your own online presence and social media assets. Very few financial institutions have started to do so.

So even though you managed to identify the 50 most important comments (this is just an example, the number varying tremendously depending on the size of your organisation), how do you plan to respond? Do you systematically respond and capture the contributors and enrich a list of key, most influential influencers (detractors or advocates, clients or bloggers or journalists or consultants)?

Data capture and business decisions

Finally, you are aware of valuable positive and negative customer comments or behaviour online and you capture that data somehow. The data is unstructured so it is tricky to process and analyse. Can you use it as part of your strategy or marketing campaign? Can you really act upon those newly acquired insights and make a business decision? This can be very controversial, as decisions by Citi and Manulife proved in 2010.

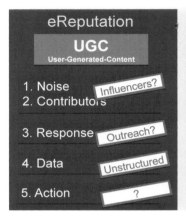
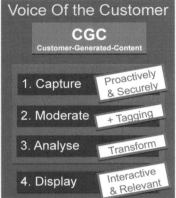

This is one of the slides I delivered in March 2011 at"Innovation, Customer Experience and Social Media".

Be proactive: urge your customers to share their feedback on your turf

Most financial institutions are concerned with negative feedback, hence they are not too interested in capturing comments and reviews from their customers. But you need to realise that your customers have access to multiple ways of expressing themselves these days. Something which they will do - they will be vocal.

You need to ask yourself: wouldn't you like to be aware of negative comments on your own turf in a close and secure environment instead of finding out like Bank of America that a video posted by an angry customer had been viewed hundreds of thousands of times on YouTube?

Wouldn't you prefer to be perceived as a company which listens and cares?

Ideally, wouldn't it be nice to let your customers do the talking and promote your products and services, especially the most profitable and popular ones such as online banking or eStatements which have an immense impact on your business?

Nowadays studies demonstrate that unarguably people trust people's recommendations, even strangers, more so than companies and their marketing messages. Even if your products or services really are the best, there are still words you can't use as a brand as it will damage your credibility. On the other hand, your customers would use their own words to talk about you, which would appeal to your prospects.

For instance your customers have their own reason not to use online banking: it seems complicated, not safe. If you could show them positive feedback from online banking customers who used to be sceptical and shared similar concerns, how much more successful do you think your adoption campaigns would be?

So listen to your clients, but social media style.

Customer focus groups are not necessarily representative of your customer base, they are expensive, time-consuming, somewhat directed, hence limiting for the contributors... Think real-time, process, long-term engagement, and innovation to improve your products and services or co-create new ones, improve marketing, improve satisfaction and drive advocacy and thus increase retention and market share.

Being customer centric is part of your strategy? Put your money where your mouth is! Start with the basics, proactively reach out to your clients and urge them to share their feedback and their suggestions.

Companies like American Express, USAA or GEICO use customer reviews to improve their products and services, fine tune their marketing message, increase customer retention and acquisition.

Customer Experience without Borders

Leverage social media to involve your customers and your key market in your product development.

A challenging 4-step approach

Leveraging VOC, looks obvious and simple, right?
In fact it is more challenging than you'd think:

1. **Capture:** first you have to capture enough data and drive ongoing contribution, then;
2. **Moderate:** you need to moderate the content to maximise its value and tag it to make the data fully actionable;
3. **Analyse and Leverage:** maximise the value of the data internally and share the right insights with the right team;
4. **Display:** display the feedback in an interactive and relevant fashion in as many channels as relevant: online (your public site, online banking, your social media presence), on mobile, or on traditional channels such as the branch network, the Press or TV.

It requires time, energy, skills and expertise, a combination that in my experience a number of financial institutions don't have.

So work with the experts, contact companies like Bazaarvoice, the leading provider of social intelligence solutions.

American Express – customer reviews on credit cards

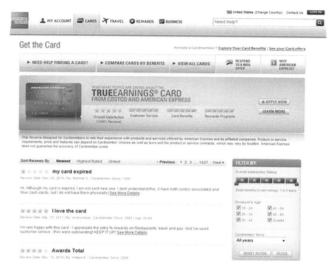

USAA – customer reviews and Q&As on checking accounts

Customer Experience without Borders

CIBC – customer reviews on online banking

Capital One – customer stories on Venture card (Facebook)

Chapter 7: Turning your clients into loyal brand ambassadors:
voice of the customer and transparency

Thoughts on transparency and social media in financial services (15 initiatives from 10 countries)

Transparency is one of my favourite topics, and it is one of the most commonly used terms in financial services, alongside "innovation".

But what is real transparency in banking in the social media age? And more importantly, which companies should be commended for their commitment to engaging with their customers and their employees in a transparent and honest way?

If you are a regular reader of the Visible Banking blog, you know how keen I am to distinguish marketing stunts from strategic initiatives focused on creating active and engaged conversations in an open environment.

I'm not against successful PR initiatives, such as NAB's "the Break Up", so long as they don't create a trend in the industry, and have senior executives think that "social media is a great tool to increase the efficiency of our campaigns and sell more products!"

I've listed the different types of social media initiatives which I believe would be qualified as "agents of transparency".

I've also categorised them into five key groups from the most tactical and the less "committed" to the most strategic and business oriented.

PR and marketing

This is by far my least favourite type as it's focused on PR and aimed to "demonstrate" how different the bank is. Again, I salute the initiatives which pave the way to more engaging activities where the customers take centre stage.

1. **First direct's Live (UK):** first direct has a great advantage over all its competitors, the direct bank provides great customer service and its customers love them. In October

2009, they launched first direct live, a section of the site where they display live comments, positive and negative, about the bank. It is good, but it lacks real engagement between the bank and its customers. What's the methodology? How does that compare with Barclays, HSBC or Lloyds TSB? What's the authenticity of those comments?

2. **NAB's "the break up" (Australia):** on Valentine's Day 2011, NAB launched an innovative marketing campaign which cleverly leveraged social media to create and sustain good WoM.

I invite you to check my comprehensive coverage on Visible Banking.

Crowdsourcing

This is an excellent way to demonstrate a willingness to listen and take feedback into consideration (as we saw earlier in the book). Those initiatives remain limited in time and the challenge is to make the most of the insights collected, demonstrate you put those suggestions into action. Ideally, create a community of contributors and find a good way to engage with them on an ongoing basis.

3. **Danske Bank's "better bank" (Denmark):** last year, the Danish bank invited its customers via its homepage to express themselves and share their suggestions on how to improve and become stronger after those difficult times. You will find more info about this initiative and Danske Bank's social media strategy in my video interview with Thomas Heilskov, head of social media.

4. **ABN AMRO's blackboard (Netherlands):** a few years ago, when ABN AMRO Commercial Banking had an innovation team, they invited their customers to share their thoughts on

Chapter 7: Turning your clients into loyal brand ambassadors: voice of the customer and transparency

online banking. The bank decided to make those ideas public. I invite you to watch my interview with Daan Josephus Jitta, Former SVP Direct Channels & Innovation.

5. **Voice Of the Customer (VOC):** There are two ways to collect and leverage customer feedback in the social media world: reactively by listening and monitoring online conversations (forums, blogs, Facebook, Twitter...), or proactively by reaching out to your customers.

6. **American Express' customer reviews (US):** in the last 18 months, American Express established itself as one of the most engaging financial services firms on social media with a popular Facebook and Twitter presence, as well as an active online community (B2B) the OPEN Forum. Since Q4 2010, American Express is displaying some of the thousands of customer reviews collected over the year.

7. **PerkStreet's tweets (US):** PerkStreet is one of the many online finance startups which demoed at Finovate. This is a new player in the US banking industry. I love the fact that they invite their own clients to respond to questions about their products and services sent by their prospects on Twitter. You need to be pretty confident that you have excellent products and your customers are raving fans, don't you think?

8. **ABSA's open wall on Facebook (South Africa):** ABSA, part of the Barclays Banking Group, has a unique approach to Facebook. Indeed, the main goal of its official page is to openly address customer queries.

9. **Progressive's moderation process (US):** Progressive Insurance leverages social media to make the most of the popularity of Flo, "the Progressive Girl", and engage with their customers openly on Facebook.

10. **Crédit Agricole Pyrénées Gascogne's "You Heart us, you Hate us?" (France):** as you already know, this French regional bank is one of the most creative banks in social media, under the leadership of their truly visionary CEO, Jean Philippe. On their homepage, the bank invites customers to express themselves, and guess the volume of negative comments vs. positive comments? 90% are negative.

Is Jean worried? Not at all, because they make sure to answer every single unsatisfied customers. So far, they've successfully turned all of them into raving fans.

Strategic

Senior executives understand the value and the importance of leveraging social media to build trust and stronger customer relationships. They are active users themselves or let their teams engage in open discussions on serious strategic topics. Their website is packed with customer generated content.

11. **Wells Fargo's the Wells Fargo Wachovia blog (US):** Wells Fargo is the king of blogging. They launched their first blog back in early 2006, and now the bank counts five public blogs. In January 2010, they launched "the Wells Fargo Wachovia blog" to cover the extremely sensitive merger between both banks, and engage in open conversations with worried employees, clients, analysts...

12. **ING Direct's CEO on Twitter (Canada):** Peter Aceto, President & CEO of ING Direct Canada is one of the most approachable and transparent senior executives in the banking industry and I've talked about him in chapter 2 of the book. He shares his thoughts on daily basis on his Twitter account.

13. **USAA's customer feedback throughout their site (US):** USAA, one of the most innovative financial institutions in

the world, demonstrates its total commitment to transparency and offers customer reviews for the vast majority of its products and services, some of their insurance products rated only 3.8 out of 5.

Financial

This is the most serious type of transparency. Here we are talking about your money. The financial institution will tell you exactly how much it makes thanks to you and how much money you'll have to pay in interest. This approach paves the way towards financial freedom and better management of your finances: no hidden fees from the bank!

14. **Wonga's representative APR 4124% (UK):** Wonga.com is a cool online service, encouraging responsible lending, which enables you to get a loan within a few minutes. They make it clear on their homepage, the representative APR is about 4124%! If this isn't transparency... I remember meeting Errol Damelin a few years ago when he was still working on the very own concept and processing engine of Wonga.

15. **Caja Navarra's "Civic Banking" model (Spain):** the relatively small Spanish saving bank gained worldwide "fame" when the current CEO, Enrique Goñi, launched the more transparent and more participative "Civic Banking model" back in 2004. In the last couple of years, CAN has been keen to leverage social media in order to take its approach online and better engage with its customers and the community projects they are sponsoring. At the end of last year, they launched an innovative Twitter contest via DMs.

So after reading this chapter, how transparent do you find YOUR financial institution?

Towards more eCommerce sites in banking

I decided to write this chapter following the huge amount of coverage Australia's Bankwest received for their newly redesigned website.

First of all, it is always a pleasure to see innovative initiatives in banking and fresh designs meant to improve the customer experience (and online sales).

Vittoria Shortt, Chief Executive Bankwest Retail, says:

> "We've looked at the best Web sites beyond financial services and used this to benchmark ourselves. We've simplified online research for customers and given them the rich experience they expect from the best sites online whilst also maintaining our unique Bankwest brand."

Happy banking

Bankwest is not the only bank to use the "Happy Banking" domain (http://HappyBanking.com.au). Indeed Bank of Tennessee in the US has adopted a similar approach quite some time ago (http://HappyBanking.com).

eCommerce, social media, UGC and VOC

The most engaging and successful brands worldwide have shifted their strategy towards contribution from their market. They understand that people want to communicate and express themselves outside of the previously almighty corporate site.

So they've been busy building their social media presence, listening to online conversations and engaging with their influencers (detractors and advocates) online. They are also urging their customers to review their products and services or share their suggestions, and discuss brand values.

And it makes perfect business sense.

Collecting customer feedback and suggestions is an efficient way to achieve a number of strategic goals such as enhancing your existing products or launching new ones (co-creation), improving your customer support and increasing customer satisfaction, or driving more qualified traffic to your site and eventually seeing a rising propensity to do business with you.

90% of the content on BestBuy.com is User Generated?

On the new Bankwest site, we are still missing the social media element and "the Voice Of the Customer" (VOC). Yes, there is a small share button on a few pages, and a big "Got feedback?" button somewhere on the site, but customer reviews are nowhere to be seen.

How much will this new design help Bankwest increase market share

http://www.bankwest.com.au now looks different from the traditional, unsearchable, self centred and opaque banking website. The industry as a whole must shift from legacy systems to content-managed systems and more intuitive, user friendly websites (public and secure by the way).

But can differentiation in banking really come from design more than the level of engagement in the Facebook era? For the last two years, UBank has successfully increased its market share based on innovative, simple and appealing products, strong customer support and better engagement online through social media. NAB was the first large bank in Australia to draw blood with its viral PR social media initiative "the Break Up".

Nowadays even though people have access to more information online, they are seeking guidance and they are expecting their bank to listen to them and provide them with a high level of assistance, wherever and whenever they need it, and help them better manage their finances. Hence the rise of Personal Financial Management tools.

People are visiting banking sites less and less due to the uptake of mobile banking (Standard Chartered Breeze), alternative payment solutions like PayPal, Peer-to-Peer communities such as Prosper.com or Friendsclear.com, and access to customer support on Twitter or Facebook (@AskCiti, @BNPParibas_SAV or @LloydsTSBOnline).

In my opinion, all those factors need to be taken into account and addressed as part of any new redesign projects, would you agree?

Other fresh designs and customer experiences in banking

Bankwest is not the only financial institution to provide a fresh, vastly improved, customer experience online. I invite you to check the five following financial institutions' websites and social media presence.

◆ **FNB (South Africa):** the First National Bank website provides an excellent customer experience and easy need-based vs. product based navigation. I've always enjoyed the level of engagement on FNB Premier Banking's Facebook page.

129

◆ **Caja Navarra (Spain):** the Caja Navarra website doesn't look like a banking site, but more like a community site with a ton of rich content and promotion of their social media presence. I invite you to check Cancha 24 (customer support and social media) and their innovative Twitter contest via DM.

◆ **Fidor (Germany):** the Fidor AG website is more inviting than your traditional banking site. I invite you to visit their online community and watch my interview with my friend Matthias Kroener, CEO.

◆ **Crédit Agricole Pyrénées Gascogne (France):** the French regional bank is one of the most active banks in the social media space. I invite you to check their site, lefil. com, which has seen a x800 increase in traffic since they started to embed their blogs on the homepage.

◆ **USAA (US):** the website of USAA, arguably the most innovative bank / insurance firm in the US, is almost all built around customer generated content. It is one of the best examples of the power of capturing the VOC in a proactive and secure way. They also built a sizable audience both on Twitter and Facebook.

Are banks ready to deal with customers like Amazon?

For the last five years, since my Head of Online Sales job at now the largest banking group in the UK, I've heard a countless number of times that banks are aiming to provide the same online experience as the likes of Apple or Amazon.

But is this what the customer really wants?

And is the industry really ready to be customer centric at last?

In my opinion there is still a long way to go, and a lot of effort needed in breaking the silos internally and shifting your employees behaviour and your corporate culture. To find out more about the challenge ahead and find some inspiration, I invite you to visit the blog of my good friend Brett King.

Chapter 8
Promotion and contests

Too many financial institutions concluded that social media doesn't work based on the fact that one or two of their social media initiatives didn't enjoy "success", mainly based on the number of followers on Twitter or fans on Facebook. First of all, it is not just about volume but the quality of the audiences and how active and engaged they are. Second of all, you must ask yourself how much exposure you gave to your initiatives. Don't expect thousands of Facebook users to join your page if they are not even aware of its existence.

So you plan to launch a contest on Twitter or an application on Facebook: the size of your audience will have a direct impact on the take up and the level of activity. Of course your content strategy (are you interesting, do you use the right syntax and call to action?) and your level of engagement with your audience will impact its success and the viral factor. But here I focus specifically on promotion.

Don't promote an online community too early like Fortis did with their then (2007) very innovative online community for European entrepreneurs Join2Grow.biz .

And don't pay for it. If the concept is great and appealing, people will follow!

A great example is American Express which launched one of the most successful Facebook pages in financial services, the Small Business Saturday page; it reached over 1 million fans in just a few weeks. Both the US entrepreneurs and the shoppers understood the value of the initiative and in this case the shoppers not only enjoyed the reward but they were happy to do something meaningful to support their local community.

By contrast, the limited take up of the Twitter contest launched by Egg Card (UK) at the end of 2010 was further proof of the challenge faced by brands.

20 Ways to promote your social media activities

Please find below 20 (smart AND free) ways available to financial institutions to give more visibility to their social media activities. I identified eight key categories.

Website

1. Homepage: PEMCO Insurance
2. Content on site: Bank of America small business online community
3. Dedicated social media page: GEICO
4. Contact page: Wachovia
5. Website footer: Net Agence BNP Paribas
6. Newsroom: first direct social media newsroom

Online banking

7. Online banking – logout page: American Express

Intranet

8. Intranet

Emailing

9. Emailing

Mobile

10. Text
11. Mobile banking – logout

Social media

12. SM cross promotion – design
13. SM cross promotion – posts / tweets

Branches

14. Branches - Windows: BBVA Compass
15. Branches - Leaflets

Traditional media

16. Online newswire
17. TV
18. Press adverts
19. Mailing
20. Billboards

My take

I personally believe every financial institution should have at least one official Facebook page and Twitter account, each with a critical size of fans and followers. Indeed, you should start by urging your employees, your digital agency, snd your business partners to join which should immediately give you a decent audience.

Please note that there are other creative ways to quickly increase the size of your fan base, such as the clever aggregation approach adopted by Citibank for the launch of its first official Facebook page, Citibank US.

So before you come to the conclusion that Facebook, Twitter, or social media in general don't work for your financial institution because you didn't manage to reach a critical size of audience, ask yourself a couple of questions: "How appealing was our initiative?" and "How much visibility did we really give it?".

Case studies/comments

Principles

Promotion: achieving high visibility

Indeed, it is good to launch a social media initiative but don't expect everybody to be aware of it straight away. Don't rely only on WoM.

Let me clarify that comment: rely *mainly* on WoM, but first make sure to promote your initiative and give it maximum exposure on your own online assets (website, intranet, online banking, social media - Twitter, blog, Facebook, YouTube)

It is challenging enough to convince your senior management of the value of social media, so don't make the most common mistake which is to spend too much money on advertising, too soon.

As a matter of fact, you shouldn't have to spend any money at all to promote your social media initiatives if you managed to connect with your members. Remember:

PEOPLE First!

Let your members, the prominent bloggers, the journalists, your clients, and (don't forget them!) your employees spread the word.

Start promoting your social media initiatives on your intranet, on your online banking, and on your public website. Your goal must be to quickly reach a critical mass of members to give a reason to your online community to visit your site, (ideally) contribute on regular basis, and promote your initiative.

Cross-promotion

Don't forget to cross-promote your social media initiatives to drive more activity and contribution from your audience!

Wells Fargo demonstrates well how to drive traffic between two of their popular blogs: "Student LoanDown" and "StageCoach Island".

And why not? There is no point re-inventing the wheel and you want to give maximum exposure to your best posts.

It is also a good way to promote (again!) their budget tool, MySpendingReport...

Social networks and services help us connect with strangers and build relationships with people from all over the world. They enable us to identify the people we'd like to meet and encourage warmer connections (vs. cold). They have revolutionised the way we search for jobs, and our ability to create opportunities with limited resources.

Having said that, telephone is good and Skype (video) is excellent, but nothing will ever replace a handshake and meeting in person. And it is such a pleasure to meet someone you've been following and interacting with online.

I've always been an advocate of leveraging social media to support your traditional offline activities, and promote your social media activities in the offline world.

Brands aim to connect with us on sites like Facebook or Twitter. More and more leading FMCG brands add a call to action to their traditional ads (TV or press) to drive traffic to a website or a Facebook page. I find it fascinating: they direct people to a social network, not their ecommerce site. That is progress, isn't it?

If we leave aside HSBC which used to mention yourpointofview.com on all its banner ads at airports as far back as 2007, and OPEN Forum by American Express which I believe last year gave some visibility to its excellent OPEN Forum community for SMEs, by and large this is not the case in financial services... not just yet. Indeed, I sense that it would take a leap of faith for any large bank or insurance firm.

You also need to keep in mind that very few financial institutions do the basics well and promote their social media presence on their own website, even the chatty and transparent Wells Fargo - Wachovia, so you can imagine on TV....

No social media promotion on TV, but what about the branches? Having said that, at the end of 2010 I was walking on 6th street in Austin, Texas (yes, walking!) when I came across a BBVA Compass branch which took me by surprise: the bank displayed a huge banner outside inviting the street passers to connect and become a friend on Facebook.

Standard Chartered UAE – go the distance

Comments

In this case, Standard Chartered is giving a huge amount of exposure on its website's homepage. Call to action: you are redirected to the microsite.

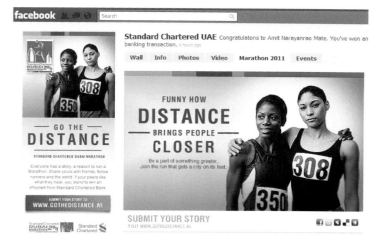

Again, Go the Distance is the key focus on SC UAE's Facebook page. The social media team updated their profile picture and, as stated before, created a dedicated tab.

They do a great job promoting on their wall some of the best stories submitted so far. They also use Twitter to amplify those wall posts.

Vancity CU – viva la resolution

Comments

Best practice – buzz / WoM marketing

This is a great example of how to engage with your community, to urge your members to contribute and promote your platform... for free.

With the Viva La Resolution! initiative, the change everything team managed to tick three boxes:

- Visibility;
- Contest;
- Fun.

Well done.

BBVA Compass – facebook's street banner

Watch the three following videos on Twitter and Facebook contests: HSBC, Santander, Lloyds TSB.

UK Banks leverage social media to target students (1/2): HSBC's Bursary Facebook Contest
UK Banks leverage social media to target students (2/2): Santander's I Love £50 Facebook Contest & Barclays' 100 Voices
Caja Navarra - innovative Twitter contest via DMs (Spain)
You can find more info on those three initiatives directly on the Visible Banking blog. The urls are available in the 'Links' section of this book (page 237).

TIAA-CREF – raise the rate

Comments

I assume the key goals for the contest are to increase TIAA-CREF's fan base on Facebook, increase share of voice, NPS, brand advocacy, and be identified as a cool brand which cares.

The contest ran from May 1 -September 28. The winners were announced on October 12. Facebook users were invited to vote for only two weeks between 14-28 September? Shame that this was the case.

As always in social media, it is in your ability to REWARD participants that determines the success of your initiative. On Facebook, your apps or contests must be fun or entertaining enough to urge users to contribute and spread the word around them.

Straight away, I had a good feeling with this contest: prizes are clearly mentioned and appealing (here the reward is mainly financial, not only for individuals but also their schools), the overall design of the page is fun, a few social media sites and types of content are used such as Twitter or video, and they made it simple for users to share on Twitter and Facebook.

- **WOM / sharing buttons:** Twitter and Facebook.
- **Twitter:** on paper, it is a good idea to use some dedicated hash tags such as #savewin and #savefail. They just need to find a way to urge tweeps to use them...
- **Facebook:** I couldn't find the app in the Facebook search results...
- **Video:** I watched the videos which are ok, but not that fun if you ask me. I am much more interested in UGC and videos from real American people. Check the AmocoFCU's earnorburn contest or the excellent Pay Yourself First Challenge by FNBO Direct.
- **T-shirts:** I wonder how many people would really buy those t-shirts. I suppose it is quite fun to give away 300 of them though.

You are using Twitter and you are participating in, or promoting, the Raise the Rate challenge? I invite you to @ or DM me to be added to the dedicated list I created.

Chapter 9
PR vs engagement

NAB's «The Break Up»: a traditional marketing campaign with an efficient social media PUSH

There are dozens of ways to leverage social media: from the less engaging (such as posting a job on LinkedIn, advertising on Facebook, using a Twitter account as "a glorified RSS feed") to the most transparent and inviting (communicating about a sensitive merger, crowdsourcing to achieve product co-creation).

On Monday 14 February 2011, Australia's NAB leveraged social media to launch a clever marketing campaign, "The Break Up" which falls into the former category. It is important to note that NAB started leveraging social media recently (summer 2010).

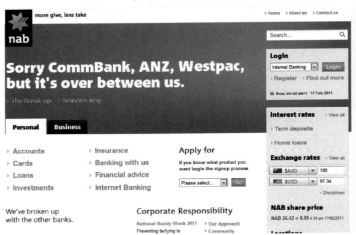

Following this my friend Monty Hamilton, former Head of Online at UBank (part of the NAB group, and one of the most engaged banks on Facebook and Twitter), sent me a DM to make me aware of this initiative. I invite you to read his excellent post entitled "Hats off to NAB... Seriously!".

First of all, well done to the NAB team which enjoyed tremendous press and blog coverage online. In that respect, this is already mission accomplished.

But in my opinion, this is merely a smart traditional marketing campaign which uses social media and more sharable content to accelerate WoM online.

Clear call to action: we are different, so switch and bank with us!

"The Break Up" relies on one key destination http://breakup.nab.com.au (some sort of blog or mini "social media newsroom") with a clear call to action which is to open a new current account with NAB.

I like the way the micro site is built: it is an aggregator of rich social media content with various feeds from YouTube, Twitter, Facebook, and a blog section listing the press and blog coverage about the initiative (with links to the original articles).

In all fairness, the bank surely has other objectives beyond driving online sales and increasing market share such as improv-

145

ing brand perception, increasing customer retention and driving customer advocacy.

NAB is the first bank to adopt such an approach, and they clearly benefit from the 1st mover advantage: they are perceived as different and (at least a bit) more transparent than their competitors in Australia.

Promotion: social media to accelerate WOM

NAB did a good job leveraging its social media assets and producing some sharable and viral content. The bank heavily promotes its initiative on their official:

◆ **YouTube channel:** a customised look and feel, a large number of videos produced for the campaign, and some excellent video descriptions with a good call to action (listing all the key links). Great results with many YouTube most watched channel awards (sponsored channel).
◆ **Facebook page:** a dedicated tab, dedicated wall posts, a dedicated discussion board (limited activity).
◆ **Twitter account:** a dedicated (generic) hash tag #breakup, regular tweets directing to their microsite, RTs and Thank You tweets to enthusiastic tweeps.

An obvious impact on share of voice and brand sentiment

I found this chart on the ZenithOptimedia Australia blog.

Again from a share of voice and brand sentiment's point of view, the campaign is a huge success. The feedback seems generally very positive and the press is talking about "a revolution". This is another proof that tapping into social media is one of the most efficient ways for brands, financial institutions included, to accelerate WoM and put a campaign on the radar of a sizable number of websites and blogs throughout the world. Surely NAB wouldn't have enjoyed so much visibility without their use of Twitter or YouTube...

Stay tuned on Visible Banking and look for my future updates (the Visible Banking Facebook Watch series and the Visible Banking Twitter Watch series): I will keep track of the impact of this initiative on the size of the bank's "communities" on Facebook and Twitter!

But social media is about engagement and conversations

What interests me the most with social media initiatives are conversations between a Financial Institution (FI) and its customers and its influencers. I love seeing FIs requesting feedback in a transparent way.

For this initiative, while I can't argue that people are talking about it on Twitter and expressing how happy they are to see a bank acting differently, I can't help but regret the lack of conversations on the bank's own social media online assets

I admit that my expectations were possibly too high, when I saw the button "Join the conversation" on NAB's Facebook page. It simply directs you to a discussion board on Facebook with only two topics and a few user comments...

Having said that, you can find comments on the wall but the bank hasn't found an efficient way (yet) to consolidate the conversations and build a real community with the contributors.

My take

I salute NAB for a clever use of social media and for being the first bank to adopt such an approach. Nevertheless, I can't help but want more from this initiative: I would have loved to see the bank engaging with the Australian people and urging them, for instance, to share their experience via a 60 sec video or a short post and collect and leverage this content somewhere (I believe the micro-site would do well).

Loads of short conversations are happening on Twitter, but the tweets are not structured (they use the popular hashtag #breakup which tag tweets on relationships, dating sometimes sexual encounters...) and the popular micro-blogging service is not a destination like Facebook. Moreover NAB's Facebook page is currently not built to capture, centralise and sustain meaningful conversations.

Will the competition step up

I'm also curious to find out how the other Australian banks will respond to this initiative and if this war of words will become their "compelling event" to really embrace social media. If it helps the industry realise the importance of online conversations, customer engagement and transparency, and become more social media aware and savvy, then great.

Social media for PR / marketing push

But I'm concerned that from now on financial institutions see social media as a formidable (PUSH) PR / Marketing tool to launch more successful online campaigns. Social media is much more than that and I hope we won't see again what happened to LinkedIn 4-5 years ago: now, most people see the great business network as a mere tool to find a job. Linkedin is much more, so don't get me started!

Transparency, banking and social media

Most tweeps talking about "the Break Up" see NAB as transparent and innovative following its launch, and I personally think it is a very clever marketing campaign, but I'd like to put things into perspective and remind my fellow social media and digital enthusiasts of some other market defining, transparent, initiatives in the social media space such as the Wells Fargo Wachovia Blog to cover the sensitive merger, Peter Aceto's active presence on Twitter (Peter is the President & CEO of ING Direct Canada) and Webank's own crowdsourcing initiative "the Wepad Project".

So according to you, how does this initiative compare?

I have a few other thoughts:

- **What's next for "the Break Up"**: this is a marketing campaign which means that it is not here to stay. I'm keen to find out how the bank plans to use all the feedback shared online, and if they plan to take this initiative to the next level and create, engage and REWARD a community of influencers. And this time fully leverage the power of social media.

- **Demonstrates the importance of building a SM platform**: NAB started on Twitter just over 6 months ago, and the bank has been on YouTube since 2005. This demonstrates the importance of building your social media presence quickly to build your audiences and leverage your assets whenever you are ready.

- **Set up new, and higher, expectations for NAB**: now NAB is the bank to beat in the Australian social media space. How will the bank respond to this status? I guess they started to demonstrate their commitment with a new Facebook page for students and a new $15m package for customers affected by the recent natural disasters...

'Lloyds TSB Me': Can LTSB emulate Nintendo's Success?

Comments

I always welcome social media initiatives and user-generated contest.

But as usual my main concern here is about the very length of this 'campaign' and the lack of real engagement with the participants: brands must realise social media drives long term engagement with audiences, as long as you keep the conversation going and demonstrate the value of your initiative. It is critical to REWARD people for (you should know by now how this sentence is going to finish, ok I'll finish it anyway) the time they spend contributing and promoting.

How little promotion?

As a LTSB customer, I haven't received any notification (neither online nor offline) about the contest. And I couldn't find any mention of the contest on lloydstsb.co.uk, did you?

I usually advise brands to fully leverage their social media assets to cross promote their social media initiatives.

Unfortunately, Lloyds TSB can't really do so on Twitter, their account being dedicated to customer support, or on Facebook, as the bank lacks an official page.

How big a reward?

I must admit that from the start, I don't find the reward appealing enough.

And I have a few questions:

Would my name appear in the ad too?

Will there only be one 'big winner'?

What about the other thousands of participants that spent 10-20mn creating their avatars?

Well I guess people in the UK are looking to prove me wrong!

So far, over 47,000 Facebook users liked the contest page and the application now counts close to 100,000 monthly users.

But is it actually as good as it looks?

First of all, success in social media is not just about how big your fan base or follower base is.

And in this case, when you think about it, there isn't much engagement after you created your avatar. At least not much engagement or contact from the bank. Basically, it is down to the participants to actively solicit their contacts.

Now let's have a closer look at the Top 6 most popular avatars (in terms of likes, but also probably commented) entries so far. We have parity with three men and three women, an avatar liked between 54-362 times.

Well done to Nikita Tighe's avatar 'Nikita' which is so far the clear leader with 362 likes and 30 comments. Please note that we have celebrities such as 'Elton John'.

I'd be curious to find out more about the moderation process (if any) from the bank or more likely its agency.

As often with this type of user-generated contests, I believe the entries lack some kind of categorisation.

If I don't know any of the participants, how am I supposed to contribute if I can't easily browse and find the most appealing one to me?

My take – focus your effort (and budget) on LT engagement

It is always good to see banks (especially the well established ones) launching innovative initiatives, especially in 'the social space'. In this case, I would just challenge the value of the initiative or the impact it could have on the brand and more importantly on the business. Indeed the level of interaction and engagement, the reward, and the approach (focused on a campaign versus long term engagement) are too limited.

A few questions to the Marketing team at Lloyds TSB and their agency:

- What is the success criteria for such an initiative?
- What's the impact on the LTSB brand?
- How valuable are the participants and how much do you really know about them?
- What's next and how will the bank engage with this new 'community' after the end of the contest?

I loved working at Lloyds TSB a few years back, and I look forward to working with the bank to help them better understand and leverage social media to build trusted long term relationships with their clients and increase customer advocacy.

But I believe these initiatives don't necessarily help the brand and will provide some ammunition to internal skeptics who believe that social media is fluffy and will never generate any business benefits.

By experience the key challenges for a financial institution, and its digital agency, in launching such an initiative are:

- **Content capture & promotion:** it's good to launch a user-generated video or avatar contest, and even better to roll out customer reviews or customer stories on your website. Nevertheless I'm afraid those initiatives won't have any impact on your business if you are not collecting enough user-generated content. You can't just rely on word-of-mouth; you have to promote your initiative(s) on your own online assets (public website, online banking, email campaigns) and ideally offline assets (branches, print ads).
- **Moderation:** in this case the potential damage is limited to the extent that the user entry is mainly the avatar. Nevertheless, people can use swear words in their avatar name (or celebrity names as pointed out above), and don't under-estimate how negatively creative people can be: I'm

sure they could come up with an avatar which may look offensive to some minorities.

♦ **Website / Facebook integration:** the bank launched a Facebook application, but the level of integration could be better optimised between Facebook and the LTSB website, which for instance doesn't use Facebook connect.

♦ **Insights and analytics:** banks are keen to prove the ROI of social media, and measure the impact of their initiatives. Very few digital agencies or solution providers provide comprehensive, actionable data and business reports enabling their clients to convince their senior management.

Chapter 10
Facebook

In May 2009, I started tracking the financial institutions on Facebook (only 128 accounts back then!). It will always be a work in progress, so please don't hesitate to get back to me to flag any missing initiatives.

As part of the Visible Banking Facebook Watch Series we are now tracking over 850 pages, groups and applications in 70+ countries: banks, credit unions, insurance firms, financial services and investment firms, credit card companies (May 2011).

In this chapter, I will share only a few best practices and case studies from the hundreds of fails and wins I have flagged on facebook in the last four years. I mentioned several Facebook initiatives in some other chapters of this book, and I invite you to find more info at http://Visible-Banking.com/Facebook.

Facebook Watch: Trends March 2010-2011

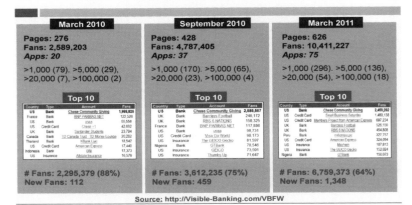

Chapter 10: Facebook

VB Benchmarking
Facebook Watch Series – Jun 11

TOP PAGES GLOBAL

Rank	Country	Type	Page Name	# Fans	Daily New Fans	Growth
1	US	Bank	Chase Community Giving	2,903,632	11,856	14.0%
2	US	Credit Card	Small Business Saturday	1,486,561	67	0.1%
3	US	Credit Card	Members Project from American Express	801,292	36	0.1%
4	US	Credit Card	American Express	681,915	3,332	17.2%
5	UK	Bank	Barclays Football	670,384	1,712	8.3%
6	UK	Bank	RBS 6 NATIONS	567,658	1,293	7.3%
7	US	Insurance	Mayhem	549,507	2,109	13.0%
8	Turkey	Bank	Garanti Bankası	406,722	3,636	36.7%
9	Turkey	Bank	Akbank	392,864	4,339	49.5%
10	Peru	Bank	mibempo.pe	352,185	466	4.1%

TOP PAGES EMEA

Rank	Country	Type	Page Name	# Fans	New Daily Fans	Growth
1	UK	Bank	Barclays Football	670,384	1,712	8.3%
2	UK	Bank	RBS 6 NATIONS	567,658	1,293	7.3%
3	Turkey	Bank	Garanti Bankası	406,722	3,636	36.7%
4	Turkey	Bank	Akbank	392,864	4,339	49.5%
5	France	Bank	BNP PARIBAS NET	118,919	51	1.3%
6	Turkey	Bank	Bonus Card	112,299	362	10.7%
7	Turkey	Bank	Finansbank	104,218	NEW	N/A
8	Czech Republic	Insurance	Generali PojišŤovna	62,852	NEW	N/A
9	France	Insurance	Zero Tracas MMA	61,127	104	5.4%
10	UK	Bank	Santander Students	52,567	10	0.6%

TOP APPS GLOBAL

Rank	Country	Type	App Name	# Monthly Users
1	US	Bank	Chase Community Giving	1,143,166
2	US	Bank	Big Break for Small Business from American Express	119,497
3	France	Bank	Mes Amis les plus marrants	54,865
4	Czech Republic	Insurance	Virtuální garáž	50,076
5	France	Bank	J'aime mon Asso	34,724
6	Ghana	Bank	iHub Intercontinental Bank Plc	26,361
7	Malaysia	Bank	Hats Off To Octo	22,595
8	US	Bank	Bank of the West Celebrates America	12,571
9	US	Insurance	iAMFAM	11,299
10	Norway	Bank	Aksjespill	10,701

Best practices and best practice organisations

FNB Premier Banking

I always use First National Bank's FNB Premier Banking page when I share my best practices on Facebook: not only do they produce interesting and fresh content, but most of the time they respond to their fans, and their CEO, Robert Keip, even spent some time shooting a video to welcome Facebook's users.

Refreshing and brilliant.

American Express

I love companies that not only started to engage on social media early and became very good at it, but also share their newly acquired expertise with their target market. It is a great way to

Customer Experience without Borders

become an ambassador for the sector, improve brand perception and increase propensity to do business with you. And after all, social media is all about sharing, right?

Dell and American Express have a lot in common. Indeed, both companies brilliantly engage on social media channels like Facebook or Twitter, and decided to share their knowledge with their small business customers. This is a clever way to differentiate yourself from the competition. We know that differentiation in financial services doesn't occur at the product level anymore, and it is your ability as a brand to be perceived as a trusted and helpful partner which makes the difference.

And currently every study on the face of the earth confirms how much small businesses need to increase their online visibility and better leverage social media.

A couple of years ago, Dell launched the popular 'Social Media for Small Business - Powered by Dell' page (with now over 45,000 fans) and American Express launched its own online community for small businesses, the OPEN Forum, with an extended presence on Facebook and Twitter.

In the last couple of years, American Express as a company decided to invest more time and resources on social media both in B2C and B2B. It is the only financial institution which has two pages on our Visible Banking Facebook Watch series (620+ pages, groups, applications in 55+ countries) and two accounts on our Visible Banking Twitter Watch series (1,300+ accounts in 65+ countries).

On November 8th American Express Chairman and CEO Kenneth I. Chenault, with NYC's Mayor Michael R. Bloomberg, launched another industry leading initiative to support small businesses in the US, 'Small Business Saturday' (SBS).

158

SBS is being presented in partnership with local advocacy, business and trade organisations across the United States.

The aim of the financial services giant is to increase awareness of the economic benefits of shopping locally at small stores.

They launched a dedicated website with a clear call to action: 'join the movement on Facebook' by liking their 'Small Business Saturday' page.

Outstanding results on Facebook, Twitter and blogs

In just a few weeks, American Express' newly launched page broke the 1 million fan mark (!) and rocketed into our Top 10 Twitter accounts.

The page, American Express' third page in our top 10, is the second most liked page from a financial institution behind the 'Chase Community Giving' page (2.5 million fans).

Twitter

Thousands and thousands of tweeps have been promoting the initiative on their favourite micro-blogging service with the hash tag #SmallBusinessSaturday, including none other than Michael Bloomberg himself (35k followers, listed 1.8k).

Online Press and blog coverage

The campaign enjoyed a tremendous press and blog coverage: on 27 November 2010 a search for "Small Business Saturday" on Google returned an impressive 1,750,000 results.

A Google blog search returned a more than decent 129,000 results.

Any negative comments?

Most blog posts and comments on Twitter are positive or very positive. But of course, we are talking about social media, right? As you would expect, you have to find some negative comments from influential people too.

I invite you to read CBS Money Watch's "Devil in the detail" column from Kathy Kristof entitled 'Small Business Saturday: Buyer Beware' which argues that the credit is limited, there is no list of qualifying merchants, and credit can be delayed.

Chase faced far worse criticism about the attribution of the $1 million prize last year when they launched their first community giving campaign. They improved the system for this year's contest.

Negative feedback is equally good, if not better, than positive comments: it gives brands an excellent opportunity to make their products or initiatives better. I am confident American Express will take it on board.

10 Reasons behind this success

1. First initiative of its kind

American Express came up with the idea and, more importantly, managed to implement it brilliantly. A unique initiative.

There is a premium to being the first, and an even bigger one if you do it right from the go! On the contrary, social media won't help you much if your initiatives are weak or old news, or if your products are not competitive.

2. A much needed initiative

I covered this earlier: small businesses need more visibility online and more cost effective leads. This initiative addresses a very tangible need from the millions of small business owners in the US.

3. Rewards for small businesses AND card holders

Even though the goal of the initiative by itself looks appealing to small business owners, American Express needed to convince them of the value of participating and spreading the word.

They gave away $100-worth of Facebook advertising to the first 10,000 small business owners who signed up to participate.

160

Moreover, to really make an impact on the economy and drive business today, American Express had to urge its credit card holders to shop at small businesses instead of large supermarket chains or other department stores. To achieve that, they promised to give $25 statement credit when they shopped in one of the qualifying small businesses on November 27th.

Please note that the offer was available to the first 100,000 enrollees only.

4. Clear call to action

As ever, the simpler, the better. American Express invites people to visit its SBS page on Facebook – this is very well chosen. People feel like they belong to something big, something which could really make a difference.

5. WoM on Facebook

Even though the Facebook page is (so far) the only dedicated social media asset for SBS, which contributed to the phenomenal growth of the page, American Express cleverly and effectively leveraged Twitter.

They urged not only small business owners but all the American people to spread the word on Facebook and on Twitter. You can promote the initiative directly from your Facebook page or Twitter account, or via the SMB Facebook page.

Please note that even though a lot of tweeps are using #SmallBusinessSaturday, the official hashtag is #SmallBizSat.

They also made it easy to promote the initiative on websites by providing ready badges.

6. Promotion – social media

I always insist on the importance of fully leveraging your own assets to give more visibility to your social media presence.

American Express did a good job promoting its Small Business Saturday initiative on its website, on the small business category page.

SBS is promoted on American Express' two other Facebook pages 'American Express' and 'American Express OPEN' with the same dedicated tab on both page and a few wall posts. They also sent regular updates on Twitter from @AmericanExpress and @OPENForum.

7. Promotion - online and offline

'A la foursquare', American Express made it easy for small business owners to promote the initiative on their website but also in their store.

Great idea, but I wonder how many businesses displayed the 'SHOP SMALL NOVEMBER 27' flyer available as a pdf?

8. Promotion - TV commercial

Once again, American Express decided to promote its social media initiative on TV.

9. Charity

There had to be a charity element to this initiative. Initially American Express said they would give $1 to Girls Inc for every like on the SBS page up to $500,000. Because of its immense popularity, they increased the limit to $1 million.

Please note that Girls Inc promoted American Express' initiative on its website via a splashpage you couldn't miss.

10. American Express

Last but not least, the initiative was a success because of American Express.

Over the years, American Express has established itself as an ambassador for the small business sector.

Moreover the financial services firm is one of the most engaged financial institutions online, and one of the most experienced on Facebook and Twitter.

This is again proof of the importance of starting to leverage social media a.s.a.p. to increase your capacity as a company to

162

constantly adapt to new means of communication and connect with your market whatever the channel.

Case study

Standard Chartered UAE

I love Standard Chartered UAE's strategy on Facebook: over the last 18 months they've done a great job building their fan base, and are constantly improving the overall look and feel of the page with initiatives such as Get Rich with a Click and Go the Distance.

At the start of 2011 the Standard Chartered UAE page reached a very noticeable milestone with over 17,000 fans.

It positions the bank as a leader in the Middle East.

Ok, the page is not yet big enough to make the Visible Banking Facebook Watch Top 10 most liked pages (SC UAE would need over well over 100,000 fans), but that doesn't matter.

Success on Facebook and Twitter shouldn't be measured exclusively in terms of the size of fan base.

It is all about the quality of the fans and the content strategy, and the level of engagement and activity on the page wall.

Very promising results for the first 'Go the Distance' campaign

Earlier in the book, I shared my comments on the Go the Distance campaign which aimed to build relationships with marathon runners, in particular the participants of the the Dubai marathon 2011 which took place on January 21st.

In a month and a bit, SC UAE managed to capture over 460 stories. Congratulations to the bank for a good level of contribution, and their iPhone winners (the Top 3 most shared and most liked stories).

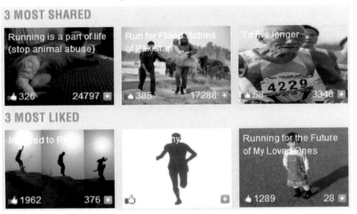

Between early December and the end of January, the bank has attracted over 3,000 new fans which could be mainly credited to Go the Distance.

In my initial post, I shared my concern about losing quality and attracting people who don't necessarily care about the Standard Chartered brand...

Please note that the Marathon 2011 tab is still available on their Facebook page.

The band new 'Services and Offers' tab

Customer Experience without Borders

SC UAE added the 'Services & Offers' tab.

There are three main sections on this area of the page:

◆ Promotion of three valuable services: online banking, e-statements and SMS banking. Not only do those three services provide a more convenient way for clients to check and manage their account(s), the take-up of those services would translate into huge cost savings and a significant, easily measurable ROI for the bank. Facebook users are one click away of liking or sharing those services on their own wall.

◆ Promotion of SC's UAE Food Explorer site: this is an initiative SC UAE launched in June 2010 to reward the Standard Chartered credit card holders.

The search engine-friendly and collaborative site invites people to share their comments on restaurants in the UAE.

The initiative even has its own Facebook page and Twitter account.

Chapter 11
Twitter

In March 2009, I started tracking the financial institutions on Twitter (only 54 accounts back then!). It will always be a work in progress, so please don't hesitate to get back to me to flag any missing initiatives.

As part of our Visible Banking Twitter Watch Serieswe are now tracking over 1,450 accounts from financial institutions in 70+ countries: banks, credit unions, insurance, credit card, and financial services and investment firms (May 2011).

In this chapter, I will share only a few best practices and case studies from the hundreds of fails and wins I have flagged on Twitter in the last four years. I mentioned several Twitter initiatives in some other chapters of this book, and I invite you to find more info at http://Visible-Banking.com/Twitter.

Twitter Watch: Trends March 2010-2011

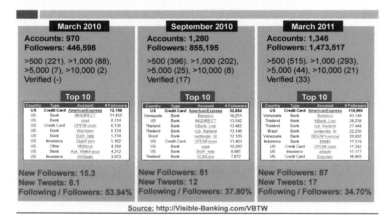

Chapter 11: Twitter

TOP 100 GLOBAL	Accounts	Following	Followers	Listed	Tweets	Verified
	1,470	1,238,454	747,609	1,981,185	83,569	54
Top 10	62,538	117,100	466,276	8,513	3
%	5.0%	15.7%	23.5%	10.2%	5.6%
Top 50	186,858	214,001	851,407	21,887	16
%	15.1%	28.6%	43.0%	26.2%	29.6%
Top 100	382,753	338,076	1,154,493	35,646	31
%	30.9%	45.2%	58.3%	42.7%	57.4%

VB Benchmarking — Twitter Watch Series – June 11

1,470 TOTAL
71 countries
1.981M followers
1.238M tweets
54 VERIFIED
4 countries

MOST FOLLOWED

Rank	Country	Type	Account Name	# Followers	Daily New Followers	Growth
1	US	Credit Card	AmericanExpress	136,587	110.6	2.6%
2	Venezuela	Bank	Banesco	56,856	182.2	10.6%
3	Thailand	Bank	scb_thailand	44,748	201.7	15.6%
4	Thailand	Bank	KBank_Live	43,740	163.6	12.6%
5	US	Credit Card	OPENForum	43,581	98.2	4.9%
6	Venezuela	Bank	BBVAProvincial	42,492	561.2	65.6%
7	Thailand	Bank	SCBEasy	26,306	118.1	15.6%
8	Brazil	Bank	santander_br	25,837	35.6	4.3%
9	Indonesia	Bank	BNI46	23,712	62.7	8.6%
10	US	Bank	ChaseGiving	23,445	404.8	107.4%

LARGEST GROWTHS

Rank	Country	Type	Account Name	Growth	# Followers	Daily New Followers
1	South Africa	Bank	CapitecBankSA	488.9%	2,485	68.8
2	Turkey	Bank	citposu4	117.3%	4,642	83.5
3	US	Bank	ChaseGiving	107.4%	23,445	404.8
4	Venezuela	Bank	BBVAProvincial	65.6%	42,492	561.2
5	Turkey	Bank	issanat	64.9%	5,111	67.1
6	Netherlands	Insurance	AEGON_NL	51.3%	2,557	28.9
7	Kuwait	Bank	KFHGroup	49.4%	9,368	103.3
8	US	Bank	BofA_Community	49.3%	2,092	23.0
9	US	Insurance	thehartford	42.4%	6,684	88.3
10	Turkey	Bank	AkbankSanat	39.2%	9,623	90.3

I focused on Twitter to make people realise that loads of financial institutions are already engaging on this popular micro-blogging platform.

Is Twitter the answer to all our customer service inefficiencies? No.

Is it here to stay? I am not sure it is going to be around forever. But it is certainly not a stunt.

Not convinced yet?

You can't argue that Twitter isn't an amazing tool for real-time market research. It would be foolish not to start monitoring the popular micro-blogging site now. As a brand, it is extremely valuable to know what people are thinking about you ... in real time.

Moreover, I really see Twitter as an excellent way to give further exposure to your other social media initiatives like a blog, a Facebook page or a YouTube channel.

One of the key values of social media and services like Twitter is to build communities and relationships. It enables brands to sustain those relationships and engage with their members / fans / followers throughout the year, even though the community is built around a special / annual event.

And vice versa, it enables brands to build relationships with customers who would only come to them once a year to renew an insurance policy for instance (by the way, I invite you to check the excellent http://vehiclevibes.com).

It is easy to set up an account on Twitter; it is more difficult to reach a critical mass of followers and engage with them in the long term. In all fairness, most of the time banks are badly advised by their web agencies, who often think about campaigns and projects and not long-term engagement.

Success: content strategy, following strategy, promotion, KYF

I strongly believe in the value of tracking and benchmarking how Twitter and facebook are used in financial services. Providing a list of Twitter accounts or Facebook pages is not enough.

Financial institutions must appreciate that if creating a Twitter account is super-easy and fast, building a strong presence and engage with "the right tweeps" on the most popular micro-blogging service is challenging.

Your success lies in your ability to produce interesting content on regular basis and make sure your content will be picked up by the tweeps you are targeting. This is assuming that you know who you are targeting? By the way, do you know who is following you?

Then you have to make sure to promote your Twitter account on your own online assets, which will make your presence more official and reassure the tweeps.

What is Your Strategy on Twitter?

To maximize your chances of being successful you need to:

1. Understand how your peers have been using Twitter in the last few years.
2. Identify your influencers (detractors and champions).
3. Design and implement a content strategy (which includes among other aspects: distributing existing content, relaying content from trusted sources and thanking your followers).
4. Promote: maximize the visibility of your Twitter account(s) on your own online assets, including your public website and your other social media profiles like your Facebook page(s).
5. Design a following strategy and a response strategy.
6. Know Your Followers (KYF): it is critical to understand who is following you, who are your most influential tweeps... In order to enhance your response strategy and start building stronger, trusted, relationships with them. The better you know your followers, the better you can REWARD them.

I appreciate this approach requires a bit of time and guidance, but it is what's required if you want to make the most of Twitter. And please don't conclude that Twitter or social media is not for your financial institution simply because you didn't see much traction since the launch of your account. In most cases, you haven't even started to really leverage this new communication channel.

Two of the most successful approaches on Twitter are: focusing on customer service or establishing your financial institution as *the* content aggregator / *the* curator for a specific topic (especially in B2B).

Financial institutions must support their customers on Twitter

Principles

You know how much I insist on the importance of your call to action, especially on Twitter.

One of the key values of the popular micro blogging site is to be able to direct a tweep to the right piece of content online in a very visible way.

An account dedicated to customer support must be as visible, relevant and useful as possible.

Misconceptions: customer service on Twitter

- Just a stunt;
- Lack of consistent customer experience;
- Not secure;
- UGC vs. L&C;
- Not scalable;
- Too resource demanding;
- Secure web-chat;
- Twitter is versatile.

What for

- Reputation management and real-time market intelligence;
- Customer service;
- Event management;
- Amplify and measure buzz for your social media initiatives;
- Sales and promotion.

Advice

- Follow the thought leaders and your influencers;
- Personalise your official page(s);
- Post between 5-10 updates per working day.

FIs and customer service on Twitter

- Start now – leverage later;
- Follow tweeple to DM them and listen;
- SM2 – smart marketing and social media;
- Deal with hacking and don't be a spammer;
- @ask_wellsfargo – best practice;

- ◆ @ubank – customer and employee advocacy;
- ◆ Twitter & ROI – success story 1 – Commonwealth Bank;
- ◆ Twitter & ROI – success story 2 – Bank of America;
- ◆ Twitter & ROI – success story 3 – First Mariner Bank;
- ◆ Innovation – banking on Twitter – Vantage Credit Union.

Case studies/comments

BNP Paribas

Comments

I would like to congratulate the BNP Paribas team for their bold move in France.

I will be tracking this account and in particular the level of activity, the growth rate, and the quality of public conversations. I must admit that I can't wait to find out how (and how quickly) some of the other banks, national or regional, will respond to this move.

Customer service is one of the most logical and valuable use of Twitter. It comes as no surprise that more and more leading banks in the US, such as Wells Fargo, Bank of America or Citi are launching customer support accounts and allocating a decent budget and resources to those activities. Their goals: to increase Net Promoter Score, change brand sentiment / perception and reduce the volume of inbound calls to their customer care centres.

Content strategy (syntax, frequency, RTs)

Principles

First of all, let's not be inconsistent here. It is true that I always urge you, financial institutions, to start embracing social media asap and launch an official presence, even if you are inactive. But you need to understand the tools and how people will pick up on your content / tweets.

Sometime ago, Susan @ Bremer Bank left a comment on my Social Media Directory in Banking, financial services, insurance to flag the bank's Twitter account @BremerBank and make sure I added it to the directory and the list of accounts I am tracking as part of my Visible Banking Twitter Watch .

Shortly after I checked their Twitter page, to find a tweet which is very unlikely to be picked up by anyone on the popular micro-blogging website:

"Stop, Go or Yield? & Much Morehttp://www.bremer.com/ Home/uploadedFiles/Shared/Investing_and_Insurance/IMT_ Newsletter(1).pdf "

As usual, I would like to make it clear: I am not saying that Bremer Bank is doing a bad job on Twitter. First of all, a sizable proportion of the 1,370+ accounts I am tracking on my Visible Banking Twitter Watch make the same mistake.

The way you write your tweets will directly impact their ability to be picked up, and the growth rate of your follower base.

It will certainly increase the probability that someone senior at the bank draws the wrong conclusion: "Twitter is not useful", or "nobody likes our content / wants to listen to us!". Let's take a step back.

How come the good tweeps out there wouldn't like content they are not even aware of?

One of the first questions should be: what is our goal with this account? What do we want to say on Twitter? And equally importantly, who do we want to connect with?

On the (very) good side, I noticed two other tweets which appealed to me a lot:

1. Using a Flip camcorder to produce video (it is cost effective and has a good human touch about it – content is more

important that how it looks like, it is more real, more "a la bloggers").

2. The existence of a social media council to share info internally, increase awareness within the organization, and identify a plan to action with clear business goals.

Delightful and very encouraging.

Lists

♦ List of Banking and Insurance Senior Executives (http://bit.ly/VBExecs)

♦ List of social media / digital bankers (http://Twitter.com/Visible_Banking/bankers-online-digital-sm)

♦ List of financial services innovators (http://Twitter.com/Visible_Banking/banking-fs-innovators)

♦ List of insurance companies and agencies (http://Twitter.com/Visible_Banking/insurance-firms-agents)

Twitter Top 10s (http://Visible-Banking.com/VBTW)

Twitter security

Principles

It is a fact that Twitter is not the most secure social media channel out there. That is why tweeple must make sure to never disclose any sensitive personal info.

It is not surprising to see most Twitter accounts dedicated to customer support reminding their followers to be cautious not only on their Twitter background but also in frequent dedicated updates.

If you are looking for best practices, I invite you to check @Ask_WellsFargo and @BofA_Help.

You surely have a process in place whereby one person logs on at least once a day to check your DMs and your updates don't you?

I invite you to watch my video focused on two of the most followed Twitter accounts on my Visible Banking Twitter Watch, @allcains and@somersetMtg:

Yes, there is a risk your Twitter account will be spammed sooner or later. Is it such a big deal? Not as long as you deal with it and you demonstrate you care about (and respect) your followers!

And don't worry too much, there are ways to minimise the risk of being spammed and the impact of spamming:

1. Check your own updates at least once a day before leaving the office;
2. Check your sent DMs;
3. Refrain from using Twitter apps which ask for your password;
4. Change your password on regular basis.

In case your account has been hacked:

5. Send an update to confirm your account has been hacked... and you are on it!
6. Delete the unwanted updates;
7. Share you experience on your blog or Facebook page and help your readers deal with spam too.

Twitter is a great addition to your customer care strategy

I still believe that engaging on Twitter with your customers is not only possible but highly valuable. Contrary to an efficient secure web chat service on your site, connecting on Twitter gives you the reach and it helps you drive customer advocacy, increase customer retention, and increase propensity to do business with your company.

And financial institutions must remind themselves what Twitter is, its challenges and its limits. Your updates are limited to 140 characters so it is obviously not made for sending comprehensive answers and engaging in lengthy discussions with your clients.

176

But it is the perfect tool to point people to the right direction and help them save time: you acknowledge people's questions and concerns, and you connect with them with the most appropriate call to action such as a URL to some existing content on your website or the direct phone number of the relevant telephone banking team.

Case study

Geojit - activity vs spamming

I invite you to watch my video reviewing the Twitter account from Geojit, a financial institution based in India and part of the BNP Paribas Group.

It raises once more the question of a centralised approach to social media versus a more flexible one.

I believe the solution lies in between: let your international entities experiment and engage with local tweeps, but provide them with specific guidelines and best practices. And make sure to schedule regular conference calls to share your experience and identify potential challenges, issues... and opportunities!

Chapter 12
KYF: Know your followers/fans

KYF is to social media what KYC is to compliance

How many of your Twitter followers or Facebook fans are already your clients? Among those audiences, who are the most influential fans/followers (activity, size of audience)? Who among your fans contribute the most frequently on your Facebook page or who RT (ReTweet) or talk about you the most on Twitter?

If you can't answer all those questions, this chapter is for you.

Earlier in my career, I used to head up the international sales operations for a leading provider of international payments routing information and anti-money laundering solutions. And a few years ago, I headed up online sales at one of the largest retail banks in the UK. This is when I got very familiar with the almighty topic of "Know Your Customers" (KYC) dear to your compliance teams and regulators, and the value of leveraging existing client relationships to increase share of wallet versus the challenge of acquiring new customers.

I will use these two experiences to articulate my post about a notion I've come up with a couple of years ago during my speaking engagements, Know Your Fans/Followers (KYF).

Compliance – understanding who your prospects and clients are

First, let's start with KYC.

This is something you have to do as part of your due diligence, before and after sending a payment or starting a new client relationship. This is now entrenched in the bank's internal processes and the bank knows that not only could there be a massive financial penalty, but more importantly, a huge impact on the reputational risk, hence the potential brand damage could be of dramatic significance and a major PR challenge to overcome.

Most financial institutions approach social media as a new type of risk. All those conversations online are perceived as a risk to the bank. The real questions should be: wouldn't it be better to reach out to your customers proactively and be aware of negative comments and recurrent complaints and fix them on your own terms instead of finding out about them on a very visible website?

After all, our business as bankers is to manage risk, isn't it? So the first step in social media is to monitor your eReputation: listen to online conversations and identify your influencers. But this is not easy and not necessarily the most efficient way to kick start your quest for user/Customer Generated Content.

Sales – maximising share of wallet of your existing customers

In sales, pretty much every single brand understands the importance of retaining existing clients, which cost far less than winning new ones. Moreover, satisfied clients will spontaneously recommend your company to those around them.

To do so, you can have sticky products, provide amazing services, the best customer support, involve your customers more in product co-creation and ask for their feedback, demonstrate your listening capabilities and your care. This is another reason to leverage social media. You must be where your customers are. And it'll increase your ability as a company to better understand the constantly higher expectations, the new tone of voice to use, and your ability to adapt to the next generation social network or revolutionary communication platform.

Leverage social media and build engaged communities (volume vs. quality)

Monitoring eReputation and building sizable communities on sites such as Facebook or Twitter are two of the biggest trends in social media in banking, financial services and insurance.

More and more financial institutions want to be on Facebook or Twitter and leverage the fantastic popularity of those services, but they don't know how to interact and more importantly how to convert those communities into brand champions or new customers.

Banks talk about volume; they launch marketing campaigns and other Facebook games to quickly increase the size of their audience, but at what cost? And what about the quality of your fan base? A bit like an internet site, if your application processes are broken as a Head of Online Sales you don't want any more people reaching the site. You may want more qualified traffic. You want to sell more to online banking customers: you know them, the application processes are shorter, you can better target them, and they have a propensity to increase share of wallet...

It has been a few years since I've came up with the term of KYF and stressed its importance in the social media space. This is not necessarily from a risk point of view, but mainly as a missed opportunity. There is this obsession with size on sites like Facebook or Twitter. Yes, it is important to reach a critical mass of followers or fans, and size matters in that respect. Nevertheless, it's better to have a smaller engaged and caring community instead of a huge audience of inactive, fake accounts and competitors, wouldn't you agree?

99% of the time, when I asked the social media or digital teams at banks and insurance companies who are their fans on Facebook or their followers on Twitter, I got no answer: how many of those fans are clients? How many actually care about the brand, and therefore are potentially excellent prospects? How many are competitors or inactive?

Much as I am adamant and passionate about customer generated content and capturing the voice of the customer, I am a strong believer in the untapped opportunity of KYF.

Especially on Twitter and Facebook: the bigger the audience, the more challenging it is to understand who those people are. Even for blogging: who spends time leaving comments? Is it always the same people?

And remember, nobody is doing it so it is still a fantastic differentiator in the hyped social media space.

Let's step back for a minute. We must think about building long term relationships, and shift away from campaigns. So how do you increase satisfaction, drive retention and advocacy, and increase acquisition at the back of it? Demonstrate you listen and, more importantly, that you care.

As usual, your goal is to identify your influencers (detractors and advocates), and start building a relationship with them as soon as possible. What's their key area of expertise? One of your first actions should be to identify and put together a list of key influencers. Then you define and implement a communications / outreach strategy to connect with them. You produce content of interest, make them aware of it. You must REWARD your fan for their contributions...

Chapter 13
Building online communities – the lessons from small and medium sized enterprises

Principles

Community in financial services is not a new concept, as the existence of a vast number of mutually owned enterprises shows.

More and more financial institutions are starting to understand the power of the internet and are looking to leverage online interactions and social media, mainly to maximise their marketing / brand investments such as sport sponsorship.

My concern is about the level of influence web / PR agencies have, versus the quality of the social media initiatives they design and launch. Banks usually experience a low level of interaction and engagement, which on occasions leads them to think community is not for them... what a mistake and a wasted opportunity.

In the last three years, a number of the most prominent online communities launched by banks have targeted the Small and Medium Enterprises (SMEs), segment. Some of these initiatives have been very successful, others less so. What explains the situation of the ones that failed? A number of reasons, mainly owing to:

◆ A misallocation of resources between start up and ongoing activity.
◆ The lack of community management.
◆ The loss of Executive support.

And off course, my old favourites:

◆ Did not fully leverage social media channels like Twitter, Facebook or LinkedIn to spread the word,
◆ Did not manage to articulate the value of their service or
◆ REWARD their members for their time and contribution.

Banks ending their communities, included:

Fortis with their once innovative community for European entrepreneurs join2grow.biz (offline since January 2009).

ABN AMRO with their Dutch community flametree.nl (offline since January 2010).

Both communities were appreciated and had a solid member base of active users.

Put yourself in the member's shoes: imagine how you would react if you invested dozens of hours on a service like LinkedIn and it simply closed down!

You must respect your members who spent hours contributing and promoting your initiative!

It is simply not acceptable to interrupt the service, give your members a few options to at least download all their data. Please forgive the repetition (and the drama), but I think that if you get this wrong you have the potential to create lasting damage to your brand.

Banks need to go into social media with a well-defined exit strategy.

Some other banks have seen their communities really taking off with the likes of Bank of America and their small business online community or American Express with their OPEN Forum. The Benche by SEB is another community that I monitor closely.

The challenges for these initiatives, like for any other online communities, are:

◆ Drive adoption of the platform
◆ Drive traffic
◆ And then drive activity.

It is an even bigger challenge for financial communities as many finance professionals are already engaged on communities such as swift's community.net or finextra's community, read online magazines like gtnews, and use business networks like LinkedIn, viadeo or xing.

Launching your own online community is one of the boldest moves in social media, requiring a much larger budget than usual (which goes with higher expectations) and more resources.

It is challenging enough to reach a critical mass of registered users, not to mention active ones.

Customer Experience without Borders

What is my template for success? We looked at some of these in Chapter 1, but here's a reminder

◆ Technology:
Don't reinvent the wheel, white label a platform from a leading solutions provider.

◆ Focus on engaging the community – use an Internal Community Manager:
The platform is not important; your ability to engage with your members is the key to success. Hire a community manager, don't outsource this important function.

◆ Think Long Term:
It will take a lot of time and effort to build an online community from scratch. You need to be realistic in setting targets, and give yourself ample time to succeed.

◆ Exit Strategy - Respect your members:
Think about your exit strategy, just in case your community doesn't take off.

Don't do a Join2Grow by Fortis, a Slingshot by Capital One or a Ideablob by Advanta which all have been wound down for a variety of different reasons.

I love seeing financial institutions trying to leverage social media to better engage with their clients or their target markets online. But I must point out straight away that launching an online community from scratch is complicated. Let's remind ourselves that not only do you have to:

◆ Drive awareness of the platform to increase the number of visits and hopefully registration;

◆ Then you have to give your members a good reason to return on a *regular basis*, and an even better reason to spend some of their precious time to contribute there instead of more established websites or communities.

Building an active online community takes lots of effort, time, budget, and a long-term vision: it would be inappropriate to close your community after just 12 months simply because you didn't manage to reach a critical mass of members or a decent level of activity on the platform.

Having said that, a few financial institutions are doing it right, for example Bank of America's smallbusiness online community or the OPENForum by American Express.

I have mentioned already that, most of the online communities launched in the banking, financial services and insurance have targeted the Small and Medium Enterprises (SME) market which is a smart move.

Why?

Entrepreneurs are seeking new ways to increase their recognition from their industry and give more exposure to their business. If executed well, an online community is the best place to network, find useful information, share with your peers, and trade.

Would you agree?

Oh yes and many entrepreneurs are by nature competitive people, so if you launch a competition you'll get entrants...these people just like competing!

But very few communities have managed to sustain a decent growth and generate consistent activity...so the industry as a whole needs to raise its game.

R.I.P. Chase +1 on Facebook. Long live American Express

I first started to write about this on 24th November 2010, but I was curious to find out how many industry bloggers and journalists would spot this too. To date (spring 2011), I haven't found any coverage of this event.

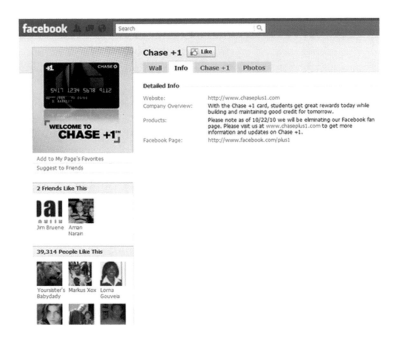

On 22 October 2010, the banking industry lost the 'Chase +1' page, as Chase decided to discontinue it three years after launch.

One of the most liked Facebook pages by a bank with close to 40,000 fans, it will be remembered for being a big missed opportunity.

The credit card industry struggles to leverage social media

In the last few years, the credit card industry has tried desperately to leverage social media. Most initiatives fell flat such as the Citi / MySpace card or Citi's clearafterhours.com in Asia. Some other initiatives had to shut down owing to other circumstances like the innovative and dynamic ideablob by the late advanta.

On the other hand, in the last 18 months American Express established itself as a serious contender to the title of 'King of Social Media in Financial Services': they became the leader in the space of both B2C and B2B with an engaged online community, OPEN Forum, and some of the most followed accounts on Twitter and the most liked pages on Facebook.

Chase +1 - how did the reward mechanism work?

About three years ago, Chase Bank became one of the most innovative banks when they launched their Chase +1 card for students.

To activate the card, and benefit from the card, owners had to be on Facebook to tap the benefits of their new card.

Remember this was before the launch and rise of 'Facebook connect'. The bank also tried to use this mechanism to improve financial literacy and drive the charity spirit among young Americans.

Please find below a few screenshots.

How appealing was the Chase +1 card according to the experts?

The card's unique reward mechanism, which basically rewards other people or entities but you, was reviewed as 'unique', but it was pointed out as potentially 'too complicated for people to figure out'. Moreover, it allegedly took too long to earn points and really make a difference. It was mentioned as 'a decent student credit card although not an all-time favourite'.

What's next for chase in the social media space?

I started to write this article on 24 Nov 2010, and the official website still invited new card holders to register their card via Facebook?

Some may see this initiative as the first step in a Facebook strategy and launch their amazingly 'successful' Facebook page and application: 'Chase Community Giving' which counts about 2.5 million fans. This year they did a great job urging people to spread the word on Twitter using #chasegiving.

The next step for the bank with regards to CCG is to:

1. Understand who those people are and how valuable this audience really is to their brand.
2. Find a way to maintain engagement between their annual campaigns.

Please note that Chase's still doesn't have an official corporate Facebook page and is not on Twitter. The conversations on Twitter are pretty negative, and I wonder if the bank has any kind of social media monitoring process in place at all?

Some of Chase's angry customers are quite vocal online: I invite you to check my video coverage of the revolt from one of their business customers "Open Letter to the Worst Bank of the Known Universe".

An explicit title, don't you think?

5 Other big missed opportunities

Chase is not the only financial institution to discontinue what could have been a formidable success in terms of online engagement and customer advocacy. The below are all discontinued online communities.

1. Fortis Bank's join2grow.biz (Belgium, closed down in January 2009)
2. ABN AMRO's flametree.nl (the Netherlands, closed down in January 2010)
3. HSBC's yourpointofview.com (UK, closed down in 2009)
4. Advanta's ideablob.com (US, closed down in 2009)

CSR-focused community by Caisse d'Epargne, beneficesfutur.fr, hasn't been active since Q3 2009, mainly because the key internal advocate moved on, further proof that social media success is a people matter, lose your sponsor and the initiative is likely to die. But it is still online and hopefully one day the bank will take it to the next level.

Put together a long-term plan and an exit strategy

When you are planning to launch an online community, the most challenging and demanding social media initiative I can think of, you must make sure to have a Long Term strategy as well as a few scenarios for your exit strategy. You must respect your members who spent hours contributing and promoting your initiative! It is simply not acceptable to interrupt the service, give your members a few options to at least download all their data.

Case studies

SAXOBANK – saxofan.net

Comments

There is no dedicated Twitter account, which is not a bad move. It enables the bank to show a different side and use a friendlier tone of voice on their main Twitter account (@saxobank), and drive the number of followers up. One might argue that may impact "the quality" of the bank's follower base.

Here are my initial thoughts:

Plus points
- Organising a contest to identify and involve fans months before the competition, and for months after
- The hash tag on Twitter, #SaxoFan
- Number and size of prizes based on success

Negative points

◆ microsite which is very "web 1.0" without any sharing features but tell a friend & become a fan (web form) page

◆ content capture mechanism: why wouldn't they urge fans to upload their pictures on Flickr and videos on YouTube, tag those pieces of content with a specific category, then send the organisers a url? Popular social media sites offer their members the opportunity to share content and vote. This translates into more buzz and WoM.

◆ reward and prizes: fancy getting your hands on "a cool inflatable #SafoFan victory hand"? Don't worry; there are still 24,187 hands left. You can also become one of the lucky daily winners of "a cool Team Saxo Bank 2010 jersey" just by posting your photo or video...

◆ winner selection process: ... but I am not sure what the selection criteria is. Have the fans voted and chosen their favourite pieces of content!

The key questions are:

How can Saxobank leverage those unique relationships to make a positive impact on the business?

How will Saxobank use that database of contacts?

How many cycling fans can they realistically convert into customers?

I wonder how many people would click on the SB Education link at the top of the screen, how many would show some interest for their TradeMentor programme?

My main question to Saxobank: how do you plan to manage this community after stopping your sponsorship? Somehow, I doubt the community would want to be merely sold financial services...

Kudos to the Saxobank team for linking the number and size of prizes to the number of fans and the success of the initiative. This is clever, and I suggest you put more focus on this aspect of your contest.

I would totally (ab)use it to drive WoM!

SEB – thebenche.com

Comments

A Marketing coup to quickly Increase its membership base?
I am not questioning SEB's motivation, the bank truly wants to create something special and provide a valuable service to one of its target markets.

Like any other community, The Benche is surely struggling to grow its member base, let alone the level of activity from the members. So I expect more and more pressure from the management to see some results. The size of the community is always one of the key indicators for senior management. I believe this announcement is more of a marketing coup than a fundamental change of strategy or redesign exercise.

Firstly the interface is almost identical for both Trade and Cash apart from the colour. Then both business areas are very close. Most of the content so far is flagged for, and presented to, both business areas.

I wish SEB the best of luck in this new milestone for the Benche, and I am curious to see the impact on the member base.

I also wonder how the existing community will react to this slight change of focus.

Your Focus is your Strength
The more focused and the more relevant, the better for a community especially in B2B.

I am concerned the Benche is now en route to compete against larger, more established, online communities for finance professionals...

Let me return to two other interesting topics: REWARDING your contributors and asking for member feedback.

More visibility for the most active members

In case you missed it, on March 19th 2010 The Benche introduced a mechanism (stars) to give more visibility to its most active contributors.

I welcomed this initiative.

Nevertheless, I wonder...

How much more visibility the best contributors will get on the platform?

What is the reward in addition to a couple of stars on your profile?

Do they plan to display the most active members on the homepage like BoA does on its award winning community?

Also, reaching the 500 comments mark seems pretty hard, doesn't it?

Excellent idea, but as of yet it needs to be more fully realised, for one thing it needs to be a bit more attractive to urge more people to contribute.

Member feedback and social media

The Benche is keen to gather member feedback as often as possible, which is a good thing to do as long as you keep your members updated and show them the enhancements to the platform based on their feedback.

I still think that SEB is missing out on social media and could make a better use of their Twitter page (only 45 followers - 25/03/2010) and Facebook page (205 fans - 25/03/2010) to increase the visibility of the Benche and its members.

It is also a good opportunity to reward the best ideas / comments, and make the most of your presence on Facebook and Twitter. For instance, invite your members to leave their suggestions on your Facebook page, and have members vote for the best ones. The winners could be featured on the blog or in the search results.

Positives
- The approach of the Benche is pretty unique in the banking industry.
- SEB market 'the Benche' on its own assets: they display a 'the Benche' banner at the top on their "Corporate and Institutions" category page.
- I love the 'Ask SEB' section to tap the company expertise in trade finance and give more visibility to its employees.
- It is a good move to have a dedicated content manager (I wonder though if Martin's job also includes managing the community, urging members to visit the site and contribute... that is critical).
- The activity on the Latest Discussion widget on the homepage indicates the community seems fairly active and happy to share.

Areas to Improve
- No or limited presence on the most popular social media sites.
- The community hasn't reached a critical mass of users yet.
- The community needs more User Generated Content.
- It looks like members don't use the 'Ask SEB' feature: the latest question was asked a long time back.
- It seems like members are not contributing to the blogs much: according to the stats displayed, there are currently 14 blogs with 50 entries.
- The calendar of events looks empty.

Unleashing the full potential of the Benche

I mean to be positive.

In fact I am impressed.

Given the current tough business environment, I was expecting SEB to potentially leave the Benche, a bit like Fortis did some time back with their visionary Join2Grow.biz, the first online community for European Entrepreneurs launched back in February 2007... a real shame.

On the contrary, it looks like SEB still values the potential offered by this ambitious and innovative initiative. They are really trying to make 'the Benche' a one-stop-shop.

It is not perfect, but I hope I have identified quite a few quick wins which would in no time take this initiative to the next level in both member base and activity.

AMEX – Open Forum 2.0

OPEN Forum 2.0 or how to reward your customers

Let's return to the OPEN Forum.

It is rare to find an online community with a simple and sleek interface, and with the right level of features.

It indicates to me that American Express worked with subject matter experts who really understand social media.

Check out the OPEN Forum for the following reasons:

1. Sleek Interface – It is clear and simple. You are not overwhelmed by too many features or options.

2. Twitter integration – I invite you to follow OPEN Forum on Twitter. It is quite rare to find a major social media initiative from a financial institution with an embedded live Twitter feed.

3. Focus on Ideas – Now, there is a clear emphasis on crowd-sourcing which I believe brings more clarity to the American Express initiative.

4. The connectodex – This feature is useful and straight to the point: find the right contact and trade.

5. Content – They partnered with recognised social media experts such as Guy Kawasaki @ alltop or Pete Cashmore @ mashable who are likely to spread the word and reach out to their large audiences of influential people.To reach your critical mass of users and attracts potential new customers, you must make your online community as open as possible and at the same time you need to find ways to give extra value to your clients. I believe it is the first time I see a community achieving that. Bravo!

6. Reward your clients – Easy Login – Amex made it easier for their clients to register using their existing americanexpress. com ID & password (it sounds obvious, but it is genius).

7. Reward your clients – Full Features – Even though the community is open to any business owners, only their clients get full access to its content and services.

I am not a huge fan of communities hosted (or worse 'embedded') on corporate websites which could be perceived as too sales-driven, but this works well for American Express.

The community even has its own URL http://openforum. com.

According to compete.com, it looks like OPEN Forum generates more traffic than some of the very best online communities in finance.

It looks like butterflies are leading the way in financial services!

Bank of America – small business online community

Comments

Today (10th October 2007), I have spent an hour on the small business online community platform.

Please find below my initial comments.

This initiative sits in the social networking space. It is a good platform, BoA successfully leveraged social network features (like blogging, tagging and rss feeds). Overall, the interface is intuitive and it has a lot to offer. There seems to be a lot of activity on the site and it feels like you are part of a community.

Can't you build your own network and contact directly other members?

But in this first release even if as a registered member you can post, comment or review articles and find other members, it looks like you can't really create a network of contacts nor directly contact the other members via the platform.

For instance, I couldn't find any security settings which would let me display my details on my profile.

As an anecdote, I found the profile of another banker who found a way past this, instead of his website he put his email address "http://johnDoe@hotmail.com". Clever. It shows that many members surely want to contact or be contacted by other members.

The goal is to create trusted business relationships, isn't it? It is one of the three pillars of the community: Connect, learn and share.

Good example of member engagement: reward your most active contributors

Recruiting new members is not too difficult but engaging them, urging them to visit the site and contribute on a regular basis is by experience more complicated AND it is critical. You need good UGC on your platform to sustain the growth and the quality of your member base.

To be successful, you need to reward your most active members. Members are giving away some of their spare time because they are seeking new opportunities. Give them more visibility!

On the UGC side, BoA do a good job engaging their members. They use good and proven features like questions/answers (Yahoo! Answers or LinkedIn Answers, an excellent way to drive regular traffic and motivate/reward your members giving them more visibility).

I like BoA's approach. The logo is present to remind you who is offering you this useful service, and yet I don't find it intrusive.

I would just challenge the link to the BoA SMB's homepage. I would be curious to find out about the journey from a community member who landed on the SMB homepage. I suspect that people could easily get lost and that the conversion rate is probably low. Especially with a small number of registered members (and an even smaller number of active members).

I would probably test a splash page with for instance a few words on the online community, and maybe an option to know more about a specific product, chat online or be contacted by an advisor.

Fortis – Join2Grow.biz

I will review Join2Grow.biz, the social network for European entrepreneurs launched by Fortis in February 2007, from a user point of view and from the view of an expert in social networking.

I am curious to understand how Fortis plans to fully utilise and leverage this network in the future... But first, they need to market it, significantly grow the number of members, and make sure their members are using it! Now, they need to MAKE IT HAPPEN!

It is an excellent, and clever, way for Fortis Merchant Bank to gather info and statistics about entrepreneurs. They can profile their members, and better understand their expectations and concerns. Their key goal is probably to build credibility, trust, and position themselves as the favourite financial partner for entrepreneurs in Europe. If they do it well, they could use the input from members to enhance their marketing campaigns, or launch new offers/financial products.

About

From the website.

Join2Grow.biz is an on-line networking community for European entrepreneurs.

Initiated by Fortis Merchant & Private banking, and conducted in partnership with TNS Sofres and McKinsey, it is the first survey to focus specifically on entrepreneurs in order to develop a complete and accurate picture of who they are and what drives them.

Their survey is one of the reasons for the launch of this network: Fortis wants entrepreneurs to access the results, start discussions & share comments, and respond to new surveys on a regular basis.

Very clever, if it works.

Homepage

The homepage is clear and very pleasant. There is a good mix of flash animation (insisting on Fortis survey) and text.

Moreover, you understand fairly quickly that the website is divided into three main sections:

- ◆ Entrepreneur survey
- ◆ Entrepreneur magazine
- ◆ Entrepreneur network

The emphasis is on the registration: Fortis wants you to register! (and I am not blaming them)

This homepage really "feels" web 2.0, it is dynamic: you see a Flash animation, several RSS Feeds, and more importantly some Tags (called "Interests" on this platform). When you scroll down, you also see some articles/posts with comments.

On the negative side, I admit that I am not a huge fan of long web pages where you need to scroll down to find extra features or options (like the Entrepreneur magazine's Channels or the "most active entrepreneurs").

Comments

Key remarks

- First, I didn't receive any notification: no email push to my personal address, not even an email to my mailbox on Join2Grow... How can they receive enough feedback if their members are not aware of their initiative?
- "we are asking all our visitors for feedback"... I assume they meant members, not visitors.
- Did they have only 1700 members after 4 months of service? ("now 1700 strong and rising") I would love to better understand Fortis key goal and expectations for their platform (number of active members? Key milestones with timeframe?)

New features and my comments to the Join2Grow team

They claim that "they have updated the layout and design, and they are in the process of adding a host of new features".

It is 11:11pm in France and the platform hasn't changed yet... New features:

- LIVE VIDEO CONFERENCES with well-known entrepreneurs

You seem very proud with that live video service. Did your member identify live video as the main feature missing on your platform? I would be quite surprised if they did.

- ON-LINE CHAT
- IMPROVED NETWORK SEARCH OPTIONS that allow you to search according to a variety of categories, including location, type of business, interests
- E-MAIL NOTIFICATIONS of the latest content about the subjects that interest you
  That's good news. It is critical to notify your members via email. And please, insist on the "call to action": urge them to share their comments or post some new content on your platform.
- ENHANCED COMPANY PROFILE that presents much more detailed information, giving you the opportunity to effectively promote your business
- NEWSLETTER summarising recently-posted articles and alerting you to what's new on the site

"We'll also be introducing more improvements and new features, such as member-created forums, in the near future." Great, at least some kind of social media features and user generated content!

What kind of technology do you plan to implement?

What is your timeframe?

We are committed to building the Join2Grow community and making it the most powerful and effective networking tool available for entrepreneurs in Europe.

This is a big challenge.

A lot of European entrepreneurs have already joined very successful, international, online business networks such as LinkedIn and Xing

- **For Fortis**: their goal is to be seen as the preferred financial partner for entrepreneurs. This network is a fantastic source of info on their target market, and if they leverage it correctly, it is an excellent (and cost-effective!) way to create new products, and support the entrepreneurs.

◆ **For Entrepreneurs:** their goal is not as obvious as Fortis... Indeed, time is money, and I see a problem.

What if I am already a member of LinkedIn or Xing, two bigger and more international networks, with members from all industries and backgrounds where I can find potential clients, business partners, suppliers, distributors, prospects, where I can recruit my future managers...

What if I also belong to some local and very active business associations such as NBI...

Why would I invest (again) my precious time on this new platform?

What would make me visit the website on regular basis?

◆ Quality of the members?
◆ Useful resources?
◆ Rich content?
◆ Business opportunities?
◆ Fame?

Launching a new social network to create a community around a key market or around a product is a very good idea, and if successful, it could lead to a significant increase in market share. But it is hard work, especially with big, well-known, "generalist" networks... As an example from outside of the finance community, Google helped Nike design its soccer community site, called Joga. com, but it does not appear to have significantly attracted users.

Conclusion

First, I want once more to salute this initiative: it is great to see a bank having a go at social networking! But if Fortis wants their new venture to be a success, they need to:

1. Market their online community.

2. Reach a critical mass of members.
3. Engage their members and encourage them to post.
4. Involve them and ask for suggestions.
5. Enhance the platform accordingly, in order to differentiate themselves.
6. Become one of the most valuable resources for European entrepreneurs.

Fortis had some good ideas, but they need to improve the platform, organise all the valuable information, urge their members to contribute, and create more value for them!

Suggestions

1. Market their online community
   I would create a blog, and have a resource dedicated to monitor the blogosphere and create some buzz (comment other posts, make sure to appear on Google, Technorati and the blog directories).
   Moreover, I couldn't find the logo or link for Join2Grow on Fortis Merchant Banking's homepage: did I miss it?

2. Reach a critical mass of members
   You are not really urged to invite more people. Unlike LinkedIn, there is no ranking in terms of number of connexions and no incentive to grow your network.
   Fortis could think of special offers/incentives to identify the best champions: they could promote a company or a service, or broadcast a commercial. Also, they should promote the members with the more contacts and display a ranking of the "top networkers".

3. Engage their members, encourage them to post
   They should organise frequent competitions (entrepreneurs and alpha types like competing) to post the most useful article on a topic, or the best advice.

They should proactively look for members willing to be interviewed.

4. Involve them, ask for suggestions
   They should ask their members for suggestions (new section, better display, new channel, missing communication feature) Again, they could organise a competition to reward the most useful/most creative idea.

5. Enhance the platform accordingly, differentiate themselves
   Create a financial advisory section: "Ask Fortis experts a question?" to create trust, confidence, and build profitable long term relationships.
   Organise offline meetings, recruit moderators, identify a few champions... Follow Xing's example!
   Off course online networking is a fantastic way of creating opportunities, but nothing will ever replace a good handshake, or face to face meetings!

6. Become one of the most valuable resources for European entrepreneurs.
   They should create a link/resource section like a directory of useful resources for entrepreneurs. (a public page with limited info, which could be referred on del.icio.us, and urging you to register to access the full info)

Other remarks and ideas

Fortis obviously want their members to use their proprietary interface to communicate (like the old AOL walled garden).
   They don't give access to contact details.

1. They should categorise and differentiate comments and questions, and ask their members to rate how useful the comments/questions are (like online communities, for example ebay or tripadvisor).

Categorise your surveys, add some content from specialised websites. Add an event section, or a calendar.

Fine tune the profiles: find the right balance between social & business

2. I think they put too much focus on hobbies and personal info. It looks "too social", and the search features aren't satisfying.

RSS Feeds

Excellent: most info is available in RSS feeds! It enables you to be kept posted of any changes directly in your feeds reader, without having to visit the website.

You have access to the following RSS Feeds:

Based on an **Interest**

◆ Most recent Comments
◆ Most active users (how does it work?)
◆ Related interests

Based on the **Entrepreneur magazine** (everything or per channel)

◆ Entrepreneur magazine: New Trends
◆ Entrepreneur magazine: Travel
◆ Entrepreneur magazine: Profile
◆ Entrepreneur magazine: Enterprise

Based on your **private messages**

◆ New messages in your mailbox - Your Private Messages

Based on the **survey**

◆ You can keep track of discussions related to a specific survey

Channels

Social media is all about user experience and sharing info: files, movies, songs...

Nowadays, the term channel is very popular. Mainly because of the fantastic success of websites dedicated to video sharing: YouTube is huge, and many other companies would like to gain precious market share in that space

Videos are categorised using tags, and could be regrouped as part of specific channels.

With the channels, Fortis wants to create a spirit, a community: they expect the members to share their experience, their advice. They started with the Travel channel, which makes sense: most European entrepreneurs travel, and are happy to find out about good hotels, good restaurants and good deals!

Podcasts

In the Entrepreneur magazine section, you have access to podcasts (text, voice or video)

I like the video interviews: quality is good, and you can directly access a specific question which saves you time.

You are invited to start a discussion and leave a comment/question.

When you leave a comment on an interview, is it also linked to an interest? How can you be aware of that comment without the specific RSS Feed?

Again comments or questions are good: it creates traffic and generates activities on your site. But members need to know they exist!

They need more channels (probably a resources/links section), and I am not sure about the way existing articles are categorised: the Have you read article is currently in the Enterprise section, which contains mainly interviews of Entrepreneurs...

The difference between Profile & Enterprise is not obvious to me.

News

I don't find the BBC World Business news feed useful. It just looks like they wanted to fill up the screen. They could have used that place for more useful links for instance, or to better promote an article based on the tags of the contact in context.

Polls

An excellent tool for Fortis.

I like the fact that it is visually nice, quick, and you can comment. On the other hand, it is messy and you need to check every single message to make sure there is something appealing.

And you have to check a couple of different pages if there are more than 5/7 comments... Waste of time. Other people that have responded -> displaying the title of the comment would be more useful. Here, I will click randomly...

Categorise your questions, and display all the categories on the first page.

http://www.visible-banking.com/2007/03/review_join2gro_1.html
Entrepreneur survey
Entrepreneur magazine
Entrepreneur network

Registration

From my laptop at home, I had some strange problems when I tried to register.

I filled in all the fields, making sure my ID was unique and my email not registered, but I couldn't go to the next stage of the process.

I stayed on the same page, with the following error messages:
- *This nickname is already taken, please choose another one.*
- *This email is already associated with another account.*
- *You have to accept our terms of use.*

Chapter 13: Building online communities – the lessons
from small and medium sized enterprises

I decided to try again from an internet cafe, and it worked perfectly well! How Weird...

Social or business?

I have nothing else to add about the profile, except that I find the positioning of this platform quite unclear: is it:

A social network?

A business network?

A hybrid network?

Sharing a hobby or a passion is a good way to create strong relationships quicker, but I think quite a lot of the questions are too personal, (although you can choose to make your answers available to everyone or not).

Grow your network

There are three different levels of status for your Contacts:

◆ incoming;

◆ outgoing;

◆ your contacts.

There are two ways to grow your network: either invite your personal contacts, or contact existing members. When you add an existing member to your contacts, you send an outgoing contact request, pending member approval.

Leaving a private message ("Leave a message" box) or adding someone as a contact are two different things here.

I think Fortis doesn't urge you enough to develop your network.

On LinkedIn, the more direct contacts you have, the more members you can reach. It is a smart way to make you want to grow your network!

Customer Experience without Borders

There is a limitation here as there is no notion of degrees of separation. It looks like now the only way for members to differentiate themselves is to be "active", which means to post a lot of comments or questions!

Search criteria: the interests

The main "search criteria" is **the interests**: an interest is like a tag. So far, they have based their search methodology solely on those tags: currently, you don't have access to an advanced search page with selection criteria such as country, city or industry...

I hope it is going to be part of the next release.

Leave a comment or a question?

Then, you are invited to leave a comment or a question? They are both identified as Comment.

The "Answers service" is quite popular (companies like Yahoo! or LinkedIn are using it to urge their members to use the website and create more traffic).

But here, I find it **messy**: the comment/question is linked with an interest. How can you easily identify the questions, and take part in a discussion if you don't have a proper title, and just rely on a tag which is quite generic?

I am really surprised they used the same categorisation for a comment or a question! Comments should be linked with a question which should be linked with a tag.

Most active members

The notion of "Most active entrepreneurs" is interesting: what does it mean?

Are they:

◆ The people who posted more comments/questions?
◆ The people who sent the most invitations?
◆ The people with the most contacts?

Chapter 13: Building online communities – the lessons from small and medium sized enterprises

I believe it is the members who posted the more comments/ questions for a specific tag/interest.

Then, they should display the number of comments per interest per user, it would be useful.

Chapter 14
Blogging, virtual worlds, Finance 2.0

Corporate blogging

In the last few years, corporate blogging has established itself as one of the most efficient, and cost effective ways to create conversations and drive brand advocacy.

Case studies/comments

Citi – blogging and bloggers

Call to action

The tag line for the New Citi blog is "Citi is Changing and You Can Help". The bank urges people to ask their questions and share their suggestions... in just 200 characters. You have to be pretty concise!

First of all, I believe it would be interesting to see the list of suggestions and questions, categorised if possible.

Moreover, I am curious to find out how does the Citi team identify the most interesting ones?

How do they plan to respond?

How those questions will impact their editorial line on the blog?

Contributors

Most of the articles were posted by "Citi" i.e. whoever is in charge of producing the content for the blog.

This is far too impersonal and doesn't fit the *raison d'etre* of a blog.

Citi should take this opportunity to give a voice to its employees and give their audience the opportunity to connect more with the content.

Even though it is great to see a post from the CEO Vikram Pandit on How Citi is changing the message is too polished and to my mind is unlikely to engage. It could easily have been written by the CEO's office...

I would like to clarify straight away that in all fairness you can't really expect to see a CEO of such a sizable banking group committing to produce specific articles on a regular basis that a blog requires. On the other hand, I strongly believe that a video format is a perfect fit for busy senior executives. Words often fall flat, and it is important to see the passion, the determination, and the leadership.

If you are looking for best practices from senior industry figures, I would point you towards Chapter 2 of this book:

Peter Aceto, President & CEO at ING Direct Canada who brilliantly demonstrates his leadership on Twitter @CEO_INGDIRECT.

I would also invite you to follow Gerd Schenkel, Managing Director of UBank, on Twitter @GerdSchenkel.

Comments and conversations

An American Banking News journalist reports that customers use the blog to complain and that some people were suspicious regarding positive comments which "might have been written by Citibank employees".

That is old news.

Any financial institution, if not any company from any industry, which launched a blog experienced the same skepticism at first. It is their commitment to post on regular basis and respond to comments which helped them change people's perception.

I know it is still early stages and Citi will surely learn and improve, but I am a bit concerned with the low number of responses posted on the blog by the Citi team. Let me use the most commented on post as an example, How Citi is changing: 60 comments were left including only 3 responses from Citi.

It seems a bit low for a blog which aims to create a dialogue and a team which promise they're listening, don't you think?

While there is yet no science or metric to indicate what level of blogging response should be expected, I still feel that the numbers should be higher.

Please note that Citi forces you to give your email address to leave a comment. Even though I doubt it happens, it means that the Citi team may respond to the comments directly via email. I still believe they should prove their total commitment by responding to most of the comments on the blog.

I wonder who moderates the blog? How often Citi checks it for new comments? And what their selection criteria is for deciding on which comments to respond to?

Even though the Citi team still has further to go, it is good to see another large financial institution blogging. And I am confident they will improve.

After all, the social media motto is "live and learn", isn't it?

There is a lot to write about Citi's social media strategy, or shall I say the need for an increasingly unified strategy and framework.

In all fairness, the size of the company makes it extremely challenging to enforce a common social media approach. More importantly, it would surely slow down everything, inertia would once more time take over, and we would still have to wait for any interesting initiatives whether on Twitter, Facebook, or blogs.

The new.citi.com blog

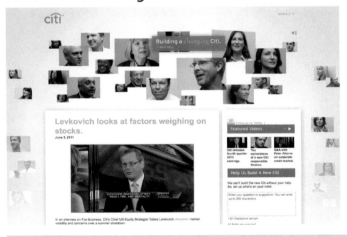

Chapter 14: Blogging, virtual worlds, Finance 2.0

As a matter of fact, the, citi.com blog launched by Citi on February 1st 2010 is one example, in my view of a large bank failing to understand social media and perhaps being too much under the control of an influential PR & Communications agency.

In this case, the agency convinced the CEO's office that launching a blog was the best way to communicate about the group strategy and create conversation on the bank own online assets... hmmm, what can I say?

I would advise against blogging on your corporate strategy or any sensitive topics for that matter.

It requires the right tone and a lot of hands-on experience dealing with UGC.

Wells Fargo – the rockstars of blogging

Since 2005, the Experiential team have been busy launching many social media initiatives in blogging (5 blogs to date), video sharing (centerstage and someday stories) and virtual worlds.

These guys definitely know what they are doing.

- *Blogging policy & guidelines:* there is (of course) a moderation process, and if you don't respect the rules don't expect your comment to be published. Fair enough.
  It also helps WF to deal with spam and abusive comments.
- *The box to leave a comment, with a picture:* genius. It makes it easy to leave your comment even if you don't know anything about blogging. It is also great to put a face on a name; it urges you to get in touch with the contributors.
- *Employee advocacy:* giving so much visibility to your employees is an efficient way to drive employee retention and employee advocacy. Your employees become "rockstars"! In this case, they have the opportunity to participate in a unique initiative in banking.
- *External links disclaimer:* icon displayed next to every external link to avoid any liability

I invite you to watch my video interview with Tim Collins, SVP Experiential Marketing (Athens, November 2008).

With social media, executive sponsorship is critical

- John Stumpf, Wells Fargo's CEO, wrote the first blog. Great way to demonstrate the blog is serious and credible. But John didn't respond to any of the comments. If you are looking for best practices for Executive Blogging, I invite you to check RaboPlus Australia's Executive Blog
- In addition to the official contributors, the following executives responded: Andrea Bierce, Customer Experience and Loyalty Director at Wachovia and Ilieva Ageenko, SVP, Emerging Trends Marketing Director at Wachovia.

Please note that Ed Terpening, VP Social Media at Wells Fargo responded to a few comments himself.

A few stats (08 January 2009)
- 5 official contributors so far: 4 WF, 1 Wachovia (3 women / 2 men)

220

- 2 category so far: "News" and a second category "History" added today
- 6 posts so far: 1 from the Group CEO, 3 from WF, 2 from Wachovia
- 92 comments so far: an excellent average of just over 15 comments per post (with the latest post added moments ago)

Marketing

- 1st blog listed on blog.wellsfargo.com
- Just a discrete text link (which didn't even make the fold) on the Wells Fargo - Wachovia Information Center

Focus on the most commented post so far: "This blog is about you"

Congrats to Matt Wadley for such a popular post which counts over 55 comments.

Matt responded to only 4 comment so far. Shame considering that initially they weren't capturing the email addresses...

1. Customer and employee advocacy

Giving exposure to your employees and your clients is an excellent way to drive advocacy and retention.

2. Negative feedback

As long as the comments fit the guidelines, you can't afford not to publish them on your blog. Transparency is critical, and having negative comments makes your effort genuine. 3 negative comments out of almost 100 comments confirms Tim's 3% theory (please watch my video interview).

3. Positive feedback

Employees, customers, and subject matter experts will be enthusiastic, and will respond to any negative or abusive comments themselves.

4. Suggestions

Show you listen, and action the best suggestions listed in your comments.

Comments

I enjoy the design of the Wells Fargo blogs, simple with clear calls to action.

For the time being, the main call to action on this blog is to visit the bank's environment affairs and green buildings pages on their corporate website, or download a 7-page pdf document.

One must say that the landing page is far from being as sleek as the blog they just left: too much text and so many links to choose from... The Green Buildings page is slightly better though.

A few words on how much I like the redesigned homepage for the Wells Fargo blogs.

It is simple, and again there is a clear call to action.

You are invited to:

◆ Leave your feedback;

◆ Follow the bank on the Twitter account dedicated to customer support @Ask_WellsFargo (one of the Top 10 most followed accounts on my Visible Banking Twitter Watch);

◆ Connect on Facebook and MySpace. Historically, WF has never been very active on those social networking sites.

Neither has the bank ever tried to launch its own online community, unlike Bank of America or American Express.

Suggested next steps

◆ WF & Wachovia should market the blog on their websites & intranet sites.

◆ The contributors should aim to respond to most of the comments.

◆ WF should demonstrate they listen to people's feedback and:
1. welcome more internal contributors who will adopt a

less corporate style (employees who don't work in the marketing, communications or brand teams),

2. create a few podcasts or webcasts (which would fit well on their YouTube channel),

3. leverage/promote Wachovia's Twitter feed (today's stats: over 160 updates and over 985 followers).

◆ Capture more info from the commentators, like BoA's Customer Reviews (employee? client? for how long?).

◆ WF should collect the email addresses of the commentators (please note an optional field has just been added).

WF recently launched a new homepage designed to better meet the expectations from both visitors and customers.

Video sharing and social networking sites are extremely popular and Web 2.0 is all about giving the power to people: nowadays, you can easily generate your own content (articles, audio, video), share your ideas, publish your comments... Your expectations have changed too: you expect companies to listen to you; you want your bank to act as a trusted financial partner.

With this re-design, WF has dramatically improved its customer experience, which will surely translate into better customer acquisition, better customer retention, and more online sales.

Well done!

ING – pickyouradvisor.com

I invite you to read my coverage of this innovative initiative launched by the late eBusiness APAC Team at ING, back in early 2007. At the time, very few financial institutions outside North America had started to leverage social media, and even fewer in the life insurance space. So kudos to ING which got back to me within a few hours and changed their internal processes following my comments.

http://www.visible-banking.com/2007/08/ings-pick-your-.html

Comments

First company to feature its insurance advisors...
It links to the media section of ING's website. You are lost, and there is no link to the original press release...

Is this link targeted to potential clients, potential employees or investors?

Basics of life insurance
I think the font used is too small, and not suited to older people. There are no hyperlinks on the pages and at the end there is no call to action. For instance, on page 13, I was expecting to find a link to the "Lifemaker application" info page on their website.

It is an interactive book. The user experience isn't great, and it could have been more interactive.

For a view of best practice, I invite you to check "the Virtual Forest" section of first direct interactive.

Download this wallpaper
Why would I do that?

Moreover, it looks like the picture is not displayed on the website... I would be curious to find out a) the reasons why they decided to add that option... b) how many times this wallpaper has been downloaded!

Get tax free income on retirement
It is merely a link to the website...

Interface – poor navigability
The interface is not intuitive and a bit messy: a lot of info or features are below the fold, the home button is at the bottom of the page... The user experience is critical if you want to drive traffic to your service, and urge your members to login frequently, be more active and contribute.

◆ A fair proportion of "community blogs" are useless: you can only see the standard "Please enter your message

224

here". Also, it is easy to duplicate your message by mistake... Before submitting the post, they should launch a script which controls the body of the message.

◆ Browsing the community blogs is not user friendly, and it takes forever to find a message which is relevant to you.

One of the key misses is the absence of categories or tags.

Tagging is the base of pretty much all the web 2.0 websites and communities. It is a very efficient way to find all the relevant info about a specific topic, share that info between members and urge them to contribute.

Registration and User Profile

Early in the registration process, they ask you to choose my advisor. But how are you supposed to choose your preferred advisor at that stage?

◆ **Add testimonial:** it is good to urge your members to leave a testimonial. But here, it looks like there is only one online! Does it mean that: no one ever left a testimonial? They received many testimonials but they were that bad? They receive many testimonials, but they don't bother checking and publishing them?

◆ **Blog rating:** this is an interesting feature. Now, I feel like I am in control. But am I rating each post? Or the whole private blog with my personal advisor? What is the impact of my vote? There is no point sending my feedback if no action is taken.

◆ **Reminders:** it is a basic reminder/alarm service. I couldn't find the list of reminders on my personal homepage.

◆ **Face-to-Face meeting:** when you click on the link, another page appears saying that you will be contacted shortly. That is it!

The Advisor profiles

◆ The way advisors introduce themselves lacks consistency.

Is the goal of the blog to recruit more advisors OR to develop warmer, more personal, relationships with clients? As a potential client, do I really want to hear about "growth potential"? Nope.

◆ I was surprised to find some personal email addresses?
◆ I would challenge the value of displaying personal photos.

Moreover, most of the time the advisors forgot to add a description. There is no checking: "Upload family photo and enter a caption".

◆ They introduce their personal background.

Fine, but I need to better understand what their approach is and find out about their key skills which could help me as a client. I need to understand how successful and popular my advisor is: it would be beneficial to have access to the number of community blogs, private blogs, face 2 face meetings, and blog ratings by advisor.

No control? It means a higher risk of brand damage
No "moderator"? Visitors promote pharmacy, Viagra, ringtones, porn...

It looks like the advisors themselves don't check their community blogs!

It does not communicate a positive image of the company. A visitor may well think: "OK it is a good service, but ING don't care. They don't even read the content of the posts..."

No promotion on ING Vysya Life Insurance website?
I briefly browsed the ING V.L.I. website. I may have missed them, but I couldn't find any references or links to pickuradvisor.com.

Social media behind the firewall
Principles

Most large organisations, banks included, struggle to share information and leverage the breadth of knowledge available internally. I touched on this subject in Chapter 2.

Most of them still work in silos.

Expensive knowledge management or human capital management systems are available, but now I am glad to see more and more banks leveraging social media technologies such as blogs, wikis and social networks.

Whatever the platform, engaging with your employees is the real challenge

With "behind the firewall" projects, I believe the challenge lies in educating people, convincing them and urging them to contribute.

As ever the platform needs to be simple and intuitive. You can roll out "the best" social networking platform, but the success of your initiative will mainly rely on the quality of profiles, the adoption of the platform from your employees, and their (valuable) contribution.

Case studies/comments

ScotiaBank – internal online community

Comments

Canada's Scotiabank announced the launch of their internal web 2.0 platform.

The "social networking" platform is based on Microsoft's Office SharePoint Server 2007.

MS SharePoint is an excellent collaborative platform, but I wouldn't describe its out-of-the-box version as "a social networking" platform. Yes, you can create your profile on your MySite section. But the bank still has a lot of customisation to do such as adding new "lists" (fields) and improving the layout...

I have spotted an interesting fact in the article: "As part of the programme, the bank is creating online user profiles for staff members."

Does it simply mean that the bank will create their employees MySite on their behalf?

Or are they going to pre-fill the profiles with basic information only or extra info available on their cvs?

Every social network's top 2 challenges are to increase its member base, and the quality of their profiles.

There is no point having a profile on Linkedin if people can't find you!

Westpac – Enterprise 2.0

Comments

"BTF projects" are easier to implement. The bank has "more control", the content is only accessible internally, and there are ways to measure **the impact on productivity** or on **the number of cross sell opportunities**.

These projects are easier to sell to your senior executives.

The benefits of using social media and user generated content internally are tremendous. Providing wikis and blogs is an efficient, and cost effective way to urge people to collaborate and increase their visibility in the bank. It helps them identify the relevant skills within the organisation and work more efficiently.

It could also help them to shine and create opportunities.

Imagine if internally you had access to a social network matching Linkedin's quality of profiles and intuitive interface... Wouldn't it be great?

You are looking for some competitive intelligence info or insights on a specific industry: what if you just had to type in a few key words to find your colleagues with the relevant background and contacts in the industry? How much time would you save?

The challenge does not lie in the technology or the platform (you can use MS sharepoint, Lotus Software, Facebook, or any kind of homegrown platforms) as long as the tools are secure and intuitive.

The challenge lies in educating people, convincing them it is worth using those tools, filling up their profile, sharing their expertise on their blog, or contributing to the wikis.

It is critical to reward your members for their contribution and their time spent online.

A social network is only as good as the quality of its member profiles and its search feature.

Personal Finance 2.0

New Innovative Ways to Borrow Money

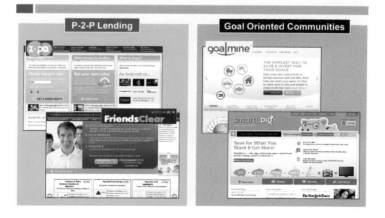

Principles

Nowadays, more than ever, people want to be in a position to better manage their money.

They want to have access to easy-to-use, if possible free, tools. They are looking for help and advice they can trust.

I believe personal finance / financial planning is currently the hottest area for banks & social media.

Proof is in the significant number of recent start-ups, and the growing number of traditional banks integrating personal finance into online banking.

An interesting statistic is from netbanker's Online Banking Report:

> "About 16% of U.S. households used some personal-finance feature at least once in 2006. That percentage is expected to climb to an estimated 33% by 2016, with nearly three-quarters of those households using personal-finance tools offered by their financial institution online."

Tools to manage your money: a good way to increase internet banking penetration for banks?

Banks want to convert more customers into electronic banking customers.

We all try to urge our customers to use the web and to see Internet Banking not only as an efficient way to check their accounts or pay a bill but as a valuable platform, customised to their needs, where they can find trusted information and purchase most of their financial products.

Truth is Banks are struggling with online sales...

A few US banks already provide advanced online financial planning tools, and I think it is a good way to:

1. Convert more customers to Internet Banking;
2. Build trust and, as a result, have more faithful customers;
3. Increase online sales.

Concept

For little or no cost, bank customers can, among other things:

- Track their spending in different categories and from different sources in one place;
- Create budgets and get e-mail alerts when they are close to or have exceeded their targets;
- Pay bills;
- Share account access with third parties;
- Transfer and store important documents online.

For more info, I invite you to check the following services:

- Bank of America's My Portfolio;
- Wells Fargo's MySpendingReport.

Virtual Worlds – a part of the mix?

Principles

Nowadays, thanks to broadband we have access to deeper, richer, experiences on our desktop.

Virtual worlds are becoming part of a global communication mix.

They are not everything themselves, they are very powerful when used in combination with the total mix of communication that you have. You bring your community into theses spaces, and you reward them: you give them richer experiences.

Virtual worlds: test new product ideas

Virtual worlds enable you to test new product ideas and new environments (like Deutsche Bank and its Q110 initiative - an innovative branch in Berlin and its equivalent in Second Life): you get real time analysis from hundreds of members, you can study their behavioural patterns, and collect feedback.

Virtual worlds: behind the firewall

Virtual worlds are extremely useful "Behind the Firewall" too as it enables people to work differently.

They don't need to travel that much, which translates to cost savings, and productivity gains. Contrary to conference calls or webex, people are more focused during the meeting. They can also prepare their meeting and continue the point they want to make online afterwards.

User generated content: an opportunity more than a threat?

Companies have a tendency to be more reactive than proactive. Social media and virtual worlds enable companies to develop collaborative spaces very cost effectively.

Even though I have always doubted the value of opening a virtual branch on Second Life (except if you are the first bank to do so), I believe financial institutions could leverage virtual worlds to:

1. Drive more collaboration internally: increase productivity and cut travel costs.

2. Provide financial education in an entertaining way: US Wells Fargo was the first large financial institution to launch an island on Second Life back in 2005, Spain Bankinter opened a branch in whyville in 2007.

3. Recruit talented people online: In France BNP Paribas is a leader in innovation & recruitment. As far back as 2007 They ran a v-recruitment campaign on Second Life and they currently provide online games such as Ace Manager or Starbank.

Even in the current context, (especially in the current context?), it is critical for financial institutions to be seen as innovative to attract the best talent out there.

Appendix

Companies mentioned

Case studies, examples and personnel featured in this book, involve the following organisations:

ABN AMRO
ASB Bank
ABSA
Advanta
American Express
American Family Insurance
Banco Sabadell
Bank of America
Bankinter
Bankwest
Barclaycard
BBVA
Binck
BNP Paribas
Bremer Bank
Caisse d'Epargne
Caja Mediterraneo
Caja Madrid
Caja Navarra
Capital One
Charles Schwab
Chase
China Construction Bank Asia
Chubb and Son
Citibank
CIBC

CIMB Bank
Clearpath CU
Commonwealth Bank
Crédit Agricole
Danske Bank
Deutsche Bank
Ditzo
Egg Ban
Embrace Pet Insurance
Family First Credit Union
FAIRWINDS credit union
Fidor AG
First Direct
First Mariner Bank
First National Bank SA
First National Bank of Omaha
Fortis
FORUM Credit Union
Founders Bank
Frost Bank
GE Money (Poland)
GEICO
Grameen Bank
Greenfield Savings Bank
Handelsbanken
HSBC
IAG New Zealand
Independent Bank (US)
ING
ING Direct Canada
JP Morgan Chase
Kasikornbank
Kuwait Finance House

Lloyds TSB
Manu Life
MasterCard
Metro Bank (UK)
Millstream Area Credit Union
MiniCo Insurance Agency
Monroe Bank
Mt. Lehman Credit Union
National Australia Bank
NIBC Bank
Nordnet Bank
North Jersey Community Bank
Novartis Federal Credit Union
PanAmerican Bank
PEMCO Insurance
Progressive Insurance
Public Service Credit Union
Putnam Investments
Rabobank
RaboDirect
Real Insurance
Saffron Building Society
Santander
Saxobank
Scotiabank
Severus Credit Union
SEB
Smartypig
Société Générale
South Carolina Federal Credit Union
SpareBank 1
Standard Chartered Singapore
Standard Chartered UAE

Customer Experience without Borders

State Farm Insurance
Sun Life
The Monticello Banking Company
TIAA-CREF
TopMark FCU
Truliant Federal Credit Union
UBank
USAA
Vacationland Federal Credit Union
Vancity CU
Vantage CU
Volksbank Buhl
Wachovia
Webank
Wells Fargo
Westpac
Wonga.com

Links

http://bit.ly/VBExecs

http://www.visible-banking.com/2011/04/tookamcom-a-social-media-revolution-in-engagement-banking.html

http://www.visible-banking.com/2010/11/after-8-weeks-and-1190-applications-from-65-countries-standard-chartered-finds-its-worlds-coolest-in.html

http://www.visible-banking.com/2011/02/social-media-policies-community-guidelines-in-banking-financial-services-insurance.html

http://www.visible-banking.com/2011/02/the-wepad-project-italys-webank-invites-you-to-help-them-create-the-best-ipad-application-for-bankin.html

http://www.visible-banking.com/2011/02/idebank-danske-bank-leverages-facebook-to-improve-its-mobile-banking-application.html

http://www.visible-banking.com/2011/05/danske-bank-launches-idebank-20-and-invites-their-facebook-fans-to-help-them-improve-mortgages-housi.html

http://www.visible-banking.com/2011/01/another-spanish-bank-innovates-this-time-by-rewarding-foursquare-users-for-checking-in-at-their-soci.html

http://www.visible-banking.com/2011/02/thailands-kasikornbank-launches-the-debit-card-foursquare-limited-edition.html

http://visible-banking.com/2009/11/bankinter-launches-bankinter-labs-micrositeblog-Twitter-YouTube-and-faceboo.html

http://www.visible-banking.com/2010/12/standard-chartered-uae-launches-go-the-distance-to-capture-emotional-stories.html

http://www.visible-banking.com/2010/11/citi-invites-americans-to-share-their-childhoods-toy-stories-on-facebook.html

http://www.visible-banking.com/2011/04/capturing-the-voice-of-the-customers-voc-are-you-reactive-or-proactive.html

http://www.visible-banking.com/2011/03/thoughts-on-transparency-social-media-in-financial-services-15-initiatives-from-10-countries.html

http://www.visible-banking.com/2011/04/towards-more-ecommerce-sites-in-banking.html

http://www.visible-banking.com/2011/03/20-ways-financial-institutions-should-promote-their-social-media-activities.html

http://www.visible-banking.com/2011/03/20-ways-financial-institutions-should-promote-their-social-media-activities.html

http://www.visible-banking.com/2011/01/bbva-compass-invites-street-passers-to-become-fans-on-facebook.html

http://www.visible-banking.com/2010/08/uk-banks-leverage-social-media-to-target-students-12-hsbc.html

http://www.visible-banking.com/2010/08/uk-banks-leverage-social-media-to-target-students-22-santanders-i-love-50-facebook-contest-barclays-.html

http://www.visible-banking.com/2010/09/caja-navarra-launches-an-innovative-twitter-contest-based-on-dms-spain.html

http://www.visible-banking.com/2010/05/will-ashton-kutcher-accept-to-join-the-jury-of-tiaacrefs-new-facebook-contest-raise-the-rate.html

http://www.visible-banking.com/2010/05/will-ashton-kutcher-accept-to-join-the-jury-of-tiaacrefs-new-facebook-contest-raise-the-rate.html

http://www.visible-banking.com/2011/02/nabs-break-up-with-your-bank-social-media-push-with-limited-conversations.html

http://www.visible-banking.com/2010/12/lloydstsb-me-nintendo-wii-socialmedia-banking-facebook.html

http://www.visible-banking.com/2011/01/standard-chartered-uae-reaches-17000-fans-on-facebook-and-enhances-its-page-again.html

http://www.visible-banking.com/2010/11/bnp-paribas-innovates-again-and-becomes-the-first-major-french-bank-to-launch-a-Twitter-account-dedi.html

http://www.visible-banking.com/2011/01/2010s-top-10-most-followed-banks-credit-card-insurance-firms-on-Twitter-1355-accounts-in-70-countrie.html

http://www.visible-banking.com/2009/11/spam-on-twitter-2-dont-be-the-spammer.html

http://www.visible-banking.com/2010/03/seb-invites-cash-management-professionals-to-join-thebenchecom-hoping-to-quickly-grow-its-member-bas.html

http://www.visible-banking.com/2009/06/happy-sixmonth-anniversary-to-sebs-the-benche-the-online-community-for-trade-finance-professionals.html

http://www.visible-banking.com/2009/07/7-reasons-you-must-check-the-newly-redesigned-openforum-the-online-community-for-smes-powered-by-.html

http://www.visible-banking.com/2007/10/visible-banking.html

http://www.visible-banking.com/2007/07/join2grow---pha.html

http://www.visible-banking.com/2007/03/review_join2gro_2.html

http://www.visible-banking.com/2007/03/review_join2gro_3.html

http://www.visible-banking.com/2007/03/review_join2gro_1.html

http://www.visible-banking.com/2007/03/review_join2gro.html

http://www.visible-banking.com/2010/03/citibank-blogging-a-tale-of-2-tales-citibank-launches-a-blog-at-newciticom-but-makes-a-fauxpas-at-bl.html

http://www.visible-banking.com/2010/04/congratulations-to-jaime-punishill-which-helped-citi-askciti-to-become-the-first-verified-accounts-o.html

Customer Experience without Borders

http://www.visible-banking.com/2010/03/wells-fargo-launches-its-6th-blog-the-environmental-forum.html

http://www.visible-banking.com/2009/01/the-wells-fargo-wachovia-blog-social-media-can-also-support-a-banking-merger.html

http://www.visible-banking.com/2007/08/ings-pick-your-.html

http://www.visible-banking.com/2008/04/scotiabank-pilo.html

http://www.visible-banking.com/2008/04/westpac-enterpr.html

CPSIA information can be obtained
at www.ICGtesting.com
Printed in the USA
2547LVUK00001B